Jean-François Lemoine

Wonderful
Provence

Translated by Angela Moyon

EDITIONS OUEST-FRANCE
13 rue du Breil, Rennes

Top : *The harbour in Marseille.*
Middle : *The Pont du Gard.*
Bottom : *Les Baux-de-Provence.*

Front cover : Aiguines

Back cover : *Tarascon castle.*

© 1986, Edilarge S.A. - Editions Ouest-France, Rennes

Cornillon-Confoux.

INTRODUCTION

Whether taken from a historical or a geographical point of view, Provence corresponds to the counties of Bouches-du-Rhône, Var, Alpes-de-Haute-Provence, and part of the Alpes-Maritimes and Vaucluse. For geographical reasons it also includes the ancient Comtat Venaissin (lying between the Rhône, the Durance and Mont Ventoux — papal property from 1274 to 1791) and the County of Nice.

This territorial unity should not mask the great variety of landscapes in an area that comprises a seaboard, mountains and the Rhône Valley. Depending on the time the visitor has to spend here and his choice of places to visit, he will see so many historic, legendary and artistic sights that it is impossible to give details of them all, nor even to list them! The area can justifiably be proud of having the desert-like rocky plains of the great Crau, the arid jagged peaks of the Alpilles, the scrub around Uzès and Nîmes, or the picturesque Carmague delta. Where else than in Provence can a one-day excursion take you in turn to see a prehistoric cave, Greek ramparts, Roman ruins, mediaeval fortresses, remnants of Revolutionary France, and modern buildings?

This guide book had, then, to be limited. It could not cover the whole of Provence and it was decided to leave aside Haute-Provence and the Riviera. It deals with the Provence of the Rhône Valley and spreads into the east of the Languedoc. The reader is presented with a geographical progression from north to south. After a brief stop in the Dauphiné, Vaucluse will be the first county mentioned, then after crossing the Rhône there will be a trip into Languedoc to visit the Gard with its landscape of scrub, before returning to the Alpilles and a few towns in the Bouches-du-Rhône on the left bank of the river. The next stop will be the Camargue and the towns on its outskirts until finally we reach the ancient regional capital — Aix.

Yet setting aside its wealth and the diversity of the landscapes and monuments, Provence has several general overall features based on its original physical and human characteristics.

At holiday time, despite the ever-increasing attraction of travel to lands further and further afield, large numbers of visitors come to enjoy what the « Empire of the Sun » has to offer. Ah, the sun! A guarantee of dry luminous summer days, of brilliant blue skies... Yet we should not forget the rain! Although it is anxiously awaited during the summer when everything is dry, the statisticians assure us that on average it rains as much in Nice (750 millimetres) as in Brest. It pours in the autumn and spring. The most noteworthy feature of this Mediterranean climate is, however, the mistral, a provençal word meaning « master ». This predominantly north-westerly wind sweeps down the Rhône Valley as if it were being pulled southwards then skirts central Provence and heads eastwards without touching the Riviera. It is to provide protection against the wind rather than the sun that the houses are built « pointing forward », with a corner leaning into the mistral. On the south side, plane trees provide shade and protection against the over-strong rays of the summer sun.

And everybody has heard of the herbs of Provence. Before they are picked for use in kitchens or to scent cupboards, the herbs' perfume wafts across the Provençal countryside. They are especially well-suited to drought conditions and to the variety of growing conditions, particularly in the scrub, a vast heath with a stony limestone soil. As to the forests, they are few and far-between today but those that do exist are mainly

pinewoods and are often in danger in summer. The Alep pine grows in limestone areas; the Maures and Estérel provide the right climate for the sea-pine. In the mountains like Mont Ventoux, hikers may come across some fine oak woods. Often, though, the landscape is an uninterrupted stretch of coniferous thickets and cypress hedges. Olive trees mingle with the vines but they do not grow beyond the Donzère Gorge in the Rhône Valley. They extend into the alpine valleys of the Durance as far as Sisteron and Digne but stop growing on the very borders of Provence.

Ageless Provence! It should be remembered that Provence gets its name from the Province that the Romans colonised from the second century onwards, while the Greeks had settled in Marseilles as far back as 600 B.C. So many towns and villages are still living museums! You do not have to open a history book to understand the importance and duration of the Roman presence, or the deep-seated religious faith of the people. The stones bear witness to it everywhere you go, be it Glanum, Orange, Montmajour Abbey, or the cloisters in Saint-Trophime's in Arles.

Regional culture is also expressed in Provençal, a dialect of the occitan tongue. It lost ground to the language spoken in the North of France as the monar-

Eygalières: *the St.Sixtus' Chapel.*

Fields near Aix-en-Provence.

chy, which had been speaking it since 1539, extended its territorial hold. Then the local language underwent a renaissance in the 19th Century thanks to the unceasing activity and published works of **Frédéric Mistral**. Today, though, despite the efforts of a small number, Provençal remains rather more a cultural language than a living means of expression for all the people in Provence.

It is also very pleasant to find the many local traditions in day-to-day life, even if they have often lost their authenticity by becoming part of festivals of folklore. There is still a strong culinary tradition as shown by the numerous characteristically Provençal dishes on offer — beef stew, veal à la Provençale, fish stew, the herby pistou soup, fish soup, and garlic mayonnaise. And they are backed up so well by wines like châteauneuf-du-pape, gigondas, or tavel! Traditional games are still commonplace, followed by several rounds of pastis.

People play pétanque (bowls), and the Provençal-style bull races are much appreciated by those looking for thrills and excitement.

And once you go home, why not continue to learn about a region which is attempting to maintain its essential balance and own culture while undergoing widespread modernisation? Take a look at the paintings of Cézanne, Van Gogh, or Picasso; all of them captured some of the Provençal landscapes. Of course, you can also extend your trip through reading works by Alphonse Daudet, Marcel Pagnol, Henri Bosco, Jean Giono, René Char, Marie Mauron or Frédéric Mistral, the author of a fine definition of Provence, « A glinting shaft of beauty on the sea of History ».

N.B. — A glossary giving the main architectural terms used is to be found at the end of the book.

DONZERE-MONDRAGON DAM

(Donzère, Drôme, 10 miles S. of Montélimar)

The National Rhône Company has now completed harnessing the Rhône between Lyons and the Mediterranean, opening it up for wide river traffic, providing irrigation for agricultural land, and producing electricity.

Thus it is that just opposite **Donzère** which was previously a mere mediaeval village that once belonged to the Bishops of Viviers, the course of the Rhône has been diverted through a dam on a 10-mile long supply channel feeding the **Bollène plant** (it is not open to the public) beneath a maximum fall of 75 ft. Beyond Bollène there is a 7-mile outlet channel. This means that the channel has a total length of 17 miles, with a width of 146 ft. and a depth of some 35 ft. It is one of the largest diversion channels anywhere in the world. The flow is regulated by locks. The maximum output from the plant is 323 MW and its average annual production of 2 billion kilowatt/hours is a French record for a hydro-electric station.

Between the supply channel and the Nationale 7 road, to the south of **Pierrelatte**, is the nuclear power station of Tricastin with an annual output of 24 billion kilowatt/hours.

From the ruined village of **Barry** (4 miles N. of Bollène) backing onto a cliff containing several of its now-abandoned houses, there is a very fine view of the Donzère-Mondragon Dam. There are other interesting views from the two bridges over the Rhône, up- and downstream from the **Donzère Gorge**, a narrow passage 2 miles long separating the plains of Montélimar and Tricastin.

St. Restitut Church, north of Bollène.

Right: *Suze-la-Rousse Castle, east of Bollène.*

Vaison-la-Romaine: *the Roman bridge over the R. Ouvèze.*

Right: *the Roman theatre in Vaison-la-Romaine.*

VAISON-LA-ROMAINE
(Vaucluse, 14 miles N. of Carpentras)

Nestling in a circle of wooded hills on the banks of the R. Ouvèze, the small town of **Vaison-la-Romaine** has an outstanding collection of Roman and Romanesque monuments to offer visitors over an area of 5 hectares. Systematic digs (which are still going on the district of La Villasse) led from 1907 onwards by Father Sautel (1880-1955), the generosity of patrons such as Maurice Burrus, and the backing provided by both the town council and the State have enabled archaeologists to bring to light remains from Antiquity, and to give Vaison (now known as « La Romaine ») a renown that has been further strengthened by the various entertainments in the **Summer Festival** and the **Choral Festival.**

Vaison's history does not date from the Roman conquest. Little is known about its origin but research undertaken by prehistorians has proved the importance of the R. Ouvèze and the geographical setting of Vaison back in the Late Stone Age. From the 4th Century B.C., a Celtic tribe called the Vocontii settled in the Vercors and Mont Ventoux, and established two capitals — Luc to the north in the Drôme Valley, and Vaison in the south. The town's name may come from that of the R. Ouvèze or from a local god named Vasio. The Vocontii who settled on the rock overlooking the left bank of the Ouvèze came downhill to the opposite bank after the Roman conquest and it was there that the ancient town was built. The Romans made Vaison one of the richest towns in the whole of Narbonnaise Gaul, and Julius Caesar even went so far as to grant it the much-coveted status of a civitas foederata, « a town allied to the Roman people ». The town layout is difficult to establish as the digs are as yet still restricted to two districts — **Puymin** and **La Villasse.**

The barbarian invasions, though, brought ruin to the community. In the Middle Ages, a long struggle between Raimond V, Count of Toulouse (1134-1194), the lord of the entire region north of the R. Durance, and the town's bishop, Béranger de Mornas, ended in the siege, capture and pillaging of Vaison. Once the bishop had been sent into exile and the local people driven out of their homes, the Count of Toulouse' men entrenched themselves in a temporary fort on the hill that had once attracted the Vocontii. It was there that the Count of Toulouse finally had built the mighty fortress whose ruins still stand high above Vaison, and it was there that the feudal town developed. In the 18th Century, the locals again moved downhill to the right bank of the river, to the site of the old Roman town. Today, new building is still going on here while the Upper Town has acquired a sleepy atmosphere and its houses are tumbling down.

THE ROMAN RUINS:

The Puymin District

The **theatre** backing on the Puymin Hill is the best-known of the

buildings and its acoustics are so outstanding that numerous events are still staged here. Built in the 1st Century A.D. during the reign of Tiberius, it is slightly smaller than the ones in Arles and Orange (the semi-circle has a diameter of 312 ft. as against 332 ft. in Arles) and it catered for 8,000 spectators! The stage and rows of seats were all carved out of the rock. It was abandoned and damaged in the 5th Century, at a time when anything that was not Christian was automatically rejected. The stone was used for religious or funereal buildings. Yet the excellent state of preservation of the machinery pits, in which archaeologists uncovered several fine marble statues that are now in the **museum**, gives a very clear picture of how the stage curtain worked. Another particularity of the amphitheatre is the colonnade on the upper portico. It has been partially rebuilt here; in other Roman theatres in Provence, it has disappeared altogether.

Further downhill, on terraces leading down the R. Ouvèze, stood fine mansions while modest « insulae » were built to the east. They were the distant ancestors of our council houses. There is a **dolium**, a vast urn for provisions, at the corner of one group of « insulae ». In the centre was the **Pompei Portico**, so called because of the discovery of a fragment of inscription bearing this name. It is a square with sides 166 ft. in length open only on two sides, where the galleries originally rested on an external wall and a colonnade. A garden ornamented with a pond and a small central building covers the vast esplanade. The walls and niches in this gallery used to be richly decorated, for the pleasure of those who enjoyed a stroll there. The north wall, for example, was decorated with frescoes and statues in niches. This is where the Roman copy of Polyclitus' **Diadumenus** was found; it is now in the British Museum in London. The niches now contain simple reproductive moulds of the Diadumenus, and of the statues of Emperor Hadrian and his wife Sabina which were found in the amphitheatre and placed in the museum.

Among the rich residences, the monumental series of rooms in the **Messii Mansion** is worth a visit. The splendid head of **Venus with a Laurel Wreath**, which was uncovered in these houses, can now be admired in the museum which also houses statues and objects brought to light

Left: *a statue of Emperor Hadrian in Vaison-la-Romaine.*

The « Pompei Portico » in Vaison-la-Romaine.

The cloisters in Notre-Dame-de-Nazareth in Vaison-la-Romaine

Right: *a fountain in the upper town.*

during archaeological digs.

The **Nymphea** is also open to visitors. It is a group of buildings around a rectangular pond that was originally covered by a roof resting on four pillars.

La Villasse District:

This district also bears reminders of fine private residences, like the ones at the end of the rue des Boutiques — the **Buste d'Argent** and the adjacent **Dauphin**. To get there, go down the main street, a large cobbled thoroughfare with pavements to either side. It takes you to the **Basilica**, which was used for all types of meeting be they concerned with business or the law. Archaeologists have uncovered a vast chamber with, on the north wall, a great arcade of fluted pilasters opening onto a small apse.

Nobody knows exactly what is left of earlier buildings in the **Cathedral of Our-Lady-of-Nazareth** which was rebuilt in the 12th Century. A dig left open in the chevet does, however, show without any shadow of doubt that it rests on Roman remains. Especially noteworthy are the nave, lit by windows pierced at the base by cradle vaulting, and the octagonal cupola just before the apse. In the adjacent **cloisters**, which have undergone major restoration, note the large arches resting on robust pillars decorated simply but with a view to variety. From there, there is a fine view of the cathedral and beneath a cornice and a frieze is the famous Latin inscription whose translation has remained such a mystery up to the present day.

The Upper Town

The old feudal town stands on the other bank of the R. Ouvèze, beyond a 55-foot single-span **Roman bridge**. It is exactly as it was 2,000 years ago, except for the para-

pet which was destroyed during flooding in 1616 and rebuilt in the 19th Century. The aim of this part of the visit is to climb up a steep path to the ruins of a **castle** built between the 11th and 15th Centuries on the very edge of the cliff. You may also enjoy a stroll on the **Place du Vieux-Marché** with its attractive fountain, or in the **Rue des Fours** with its fine houses that were restored some twenty years ago.

MONT VENTOUX
(Vaucluse, 19 miles N-E. of Carpentras)

At 6,208 feet, **Mont Ventoux** is the highest point in the Rhône Valley area of Provence. It stands between the Baronnies and Ouvèze rivers to the north, and the Saint-Christol plain and Lubéron chain to the south. Whatever the season, it provides nature-lovers and sportsmen with a unique place for an outing.

Before reaching the summit which is swept by strong winds and carpeted with white stones, walkers are faced with an infinite horizon in a quite magnificent natural setting. As they climb, they come across various levels of vegetation and many different varieties of tree. Botanists will find something to get their teeth into; they may even find polar flowers at the summit (certain species of saxifrage or the Iceland poppy). The mountainsides are covered with pines, green oaks, cedars, beech, firs, and larch. Cyclists taking part in the Tour de France and car hill-climb enthusiasts can all be found here, as can skiers on **Mont Serein**. As to the summit, it is the site of a National Met. Office observatory, an Army radar station, and a T.V. transmitter.

THE DENTELLES DE MONTMIRAIL
(Vaucluse, 7 miles N. of Carpentras)

The **Dentelles de Montmirail**, the last outcrop of Mont Ventoux, stretching from **Gigondas** to **Malaucène**, owe their name to their unusual appearance. The strange limestone peaks that erosion has made so jagged are reminiscent of a piece of brilliant white lace.

Although their summit, the **Pic Saint-Amand**, is at only 239 ft., their geographical relief is very marked and they attract all those who enjoy

Top: *the Dentelles de Montmirail.*
Bottom left: *the village of Crestet near Vaison.*
Bottom right: *an agricultural landscape near Gigondas.*

Mont Ventoux seen from the Vaucluse Plateau.

outings and walking. A fine road through the **Col de Cayron** (1,287 ft.) wends its way through a landscape of pines and oaks. The drive is made all the more enjoyable by the stops enabling visitors to taste one of the famous côtes-du-Rhône wines — gigondas, a red wine that was already popular in Roman days. Nor should we forget the muscat produced in **Beaumes-de-Venise** on the lower slopes of the Dentelles.

ORANGE
(Vaucluse, 17 miles N. of Avignon)

In 105 B.C., the Celtic settlement of Arausio entered the pages of the history books, before it became a Roman colony. It was beneath its walls that the Cimbrians and Teutons routed Consul Manlius' troops, massacring more than 100,000 legionaries. It was, though, in 36 B.C. that the town finally threw in its lot with Rome and, during the period of « pax romana », the highly-prosperous **Orange** was densely populated (it had four times as many inhabitants as it has today!) and had many large public buildings — a theatre, amphitheatre, temples, baths, triumphal arch, circus, gymnasium etc. After being pillaged by the Alamanns and the Visigoths, it became the capital of a principality in the 13th Century. The chance conditions of an inheritance in 1530 made it Dutch, and it was governed by the Nassau family until 1731 when it was finally reunited with France. It was indeed William of Nassau, known as « William the Taciturn », who created the Republic of United Provinces in the Netherlands. Geographical distance did not prevent successive princes from taking an interest in their French territory. In 1622, Maurice of Nassau fortified the town and gave it a castle, using what Roman building materials had not been destroyed by the barbarians. All that was left were the theatre and the triumphal arch. Castle and town walls were to be razed to the ground in their turn, however, when Louis XIV declared

The south side of the municipal arch in Orange.

Left: *the western basilica in the Roman theatre in Orange.*

war on Holland. Surrounded on all sides by the comtat Venaissin, it was to be included in the county of Vaucluse at the same time, in 1791.

The **ancient theatre** which, since 1869, has housed the world-famous « **Chorégies** » festival specialising in opera, is the best-preserved of its kind anywhere in the Roman world. It was the centre of daily life in Gallo-Roman times. As foundations for the theatre, the architect used the steep slope of the hillside.

Seen from the outside, it consists of a series of semi-circular arches flanked by pilasters and topped by the blind arcading that served as architectural decoration. On the upper level, two rows of stones jutting out from the wall were used to anchor the masts on which an awning was stretched to provide spectators with protection from the sun and bad weather. Inside, the **huge back-wall** of the stage is especially admirable, «the finest wall in the kingdom of France» as Louis XIV

17

The inside of the Roman theatre in Orange.

Top right: *the municipal arch in Orange - a panel of arms to the south-east.*

Bottom right: *the municipal arch, bas-reliefs on the upper section of the attic.*

called it. It is 335 ft. long and 120 ft. wide and it stands intact in the vast semicircle 390 ft. in diameter. Above the central doorway was a freize of centaurs which has since disappeared. In the great niche towering over the entire building stands the copy of the **statue of Augustus** 11 1/2 ft. high. Dressed in armour and wearing the imperial toga, he salutes the crowd of spectators while on his right kneels a defeated man who was no doubt depicted imploring his mercy. The theatre, which can now hold an audience of 7,000, originally catered for 11,000 spectators. Its acoustics are still excellent.

Just nearby, across a **paved street**, are some puzzling **remains**. Inscriptions mention a capitol and temples, but only the **Capitol** has been traced, on St. Eutropius' Hill,

a vast platform where three temples are thought once to have stood. Halfway up the hill, there was an-other temple whose remains were uncovered during the building of the town's water tower. It was razed to the ground in the 2nd Century and replaced by a colossal temple of which the **podium** still remains, in the midst of the huge paved enclosure. It was first thought that the original monument was built to finish off a circus, then it was believed to have been part of a gymnasium. Today, archaeologists are of the opinion that it was more likely to have been a gigantic **nymphea** decorated with ponds, waterfalls and statues. A hypothesis that is yet to be proven...

The **triumphal arch** in the north of the town was the town's main

gate during the imperial era and was the symbol of Roman might for all those who passed beneath it. It is one of the oldest triple arches and is believed to have been built before 26-27 A.D. It was originally a municipal archway celebrating the exploits of the Second Gallic Legion (the legion's emblem, a double capricorn, can be seen on one of the carved shields), before being dedicated to Tiberius. It is unusual for the pediment above the central façade. Among the profusion of decorative features, there are scenes of battle against the Gauls on the attic, reminders of Caesar's naval victories beside the tympanum, and prisoners in chains and panels of weapons on one side. The archway is 72 ft. high, 69 ft. wide, and 26 ft. deep.

FONTAINE-DE-VAUCLUSE
(Vaucluse, 11 miles N. of Cavaillon)

« Already famous for its wonders », wrote Petrarch, « Vaucluse has become even more so through my long stay there and through my songs ». And it is quite true that, for the million visitors who come here every year, the beauty of this picturesque spot merges with memories of the great Italian poet (1304-1374). He first met the woman whose prasies he sang in his Canzoniere, Laure de Noves, in a church in Avignon on 6th April 1327. In the grip of a violent but hopeless love, he lived as a recluse in Vaucluse for sixteen years from 1337 to 1353, at the invitation of the Bishop of Cavaillon, Philippe de Cabassol.

The lady of his every thought, the wife of Hugues de Sade, died of the plague in Avignon on the same date, April 6th, but twenty-one years later. As to the poet, whose feelings were still as passionate, he lived for a further twenty years and died near Padua.

A **commemorative column** (dating from 1804) was erected on the occasion of the five hundredth anniversary of his birth. A **museum** in a house said to have been built on the site of the one occupied by the poet has some beautiful editions of his works in an exhibition on the first floor. Also worth a visit are the **castle** built on top of a rock, which once belonged to the Bishops of Cavaillon, and the Romanesque **St. Véran's Church** (11th

Left: *the Petrarch Column in Fontaine-de-Vaucluse.*

St. Véran Church.

Century). In its crypt is the sarcophagus of St. Véran, Bishop of Cavaillon in the 6th Century.

The source of the R. Sorgue, one of the most powerful springs anywhere in the world, gushes from a grotto in the depths of a rocky cwm with scarp slopes on all sides. It is the overflow of a large underground river fed by rainwater from the Vaucluse Plateau, Mont Ventoux, the Lubéron, and the Lure Montain. Unfortunately, the entire course of the river has never been charted despite numerous attempts, including one by Commandant Cousteau. During high water, in winter or spring, the rate of flow can be as much as 150-200 m³/sec. while in summer it falls to 8 m³/sec. When the river is in full spate, you may be lucky enough to see the impressive spectacle of emerald-green water rushing over the surrounding rocks.

A waterwheel in l'Isle-sur-la-Sorgue.

R. Sorgue in Fontaine-de-Vaucluse.

SENANQUE ABBEY
(Vaucluse, 13 miles N-W. of Apt)

The Cistercian abbey of Sénanque is the last of the « three Provençal sisters » (Le Thoronet built in 1136, and Silvacane in 1147) since the building was begun here in 1148, in a narrow valley near Gordes, by monks from Mazan in Ardèche. The powerful Simian family contributed to the founding of this austere edifice with its stark architecture, a sobriety that is a perfect reflection of the Cistercian monks' will for purity and poverty.

Today, most of the 12th-century buildings are open to the public. At that time, the abbey had approximately twelve monks. The only exceptions are the refectory and the building used by the lay brothers, both of which were burnt down in 1544 by Vaudois rebels. Sold off as State property during the Revolution to Mr. de Léouze, a man of independant means from Aix, the abbey was reoccupied from 1854 until the end of the 19th Century, and from 1926 to 1969 when the monks returned to the île de Lérins.

At the present time, Sénanque is a very lively cultural centre (with concerts of plainsong and mediaeval music) which also houses a foundation dedicated to the Sahara containing several very rich collections.

Because of the layout of this spot (the **Sénancole Valley** has very steep sides), the builders had to erect the chevet of the church at the east end of the other buildings, and not on the north side as is usual. The **church** in the shape of a Latin cross is remarkable for the beauty of its ribbed cradle vault and for the absence of any interior decoration.

From top to bottom: *a general view of the abbey, the cloisters, the chapter house.*

Overleaf: *the chevet of Sénanque Abbey and the lavender fields in springtime.*

The belltower, which is reminiscent of the ones in Silvacane and Saint-Michel-de-Frigolet, is a stocky square turret topped by a pyramid. The heart of the monastery, and the place for reading and meditation, was the **cloister**, a courtyard surrounded by four galleries. Visitors cannot fail to admire the capitals on the colonettes, carved with a variety of foliage and floral motifs. Also open to the public are the **dorter** with its magnificent Romanesque ribbed barrel vault, the **calefactory**, the **chapter house** where the community used to assemble, and the **refectory**. The later buildings now house the cultural centre — reception rooms, exhibitions halls, and accommodation.

Right, from top to bottom: *the façade of the church, a capital in the cloisters, the nave in Sénanque Church.*

Below: *the chancel of Sénanque Church.*

GORDES
(Vaucluse, 13 miles N-W. of Apt)

The best view of this picturesque village is to be had from the Cavaillon road. Gordes, on the edge of the plateau overlooking the **Coulon Plain**, was built on a craggy promontory on whose slopes stand rows of dry-stone houses. From their midst there emerges the **Church of the Assumption** (18th Century) and the Renaissance castle flanked by two round towers with large machicolations. Designed by Bertrand de Simiane, this huge construction was built on the site of a mediaeval fortress. In the courtyard, your eye will automatically be drawn to a beautiful door with Renaissance decoration, and you will also be impressed by the multitude of ornamentation on the fireplace in the great chamber on the first floor. Five of the castle's rooms have been used since 1970 to house the **Vasarély Museum** presenting geometric-style paintings and decorative panels. This is an opportunity to admire one of the modern points of contact between Art and Science.

Just over one mile from Gordes on the Cavaillon road, beyond a belvedere offering visitors a fine view of the village, is the **Black Village** which has been abandoned for several centuries. It is also known as the Village of Bories because it includes some ten of these strange limestone buildings. The huts are usually circular, the largest ones having several rooms; they look like dry stone « igloos ». Today it is still not known when the first ones were built. What is known for sure, however, is that they were used as housing until the 19th Century.

SILVACANE ABBEY
(Bouches-du-Rhône, 24 miles S-E. of Cavaillon)

Not far from the R. Durance in the midst of vineyards stands the Romanesque Abbey of Silvacane. Founded in 1144, it received donations from the lords of Les Baux who wished to be buried there. In the north chapel of the apse, there are fragments of the tomb of Bertrand de Baux who ordered building work to begin on the church in 1175. The work undertaken by monks from Morimond (in Champagne) made slow progress; the cloisters were not finished until the end of the 13th Century.

After a period of prosperity that lasted until 1357, the abbey had a series of ups and downs. The One Hundred Years' War was followed by rivalry between Silvacane and Montmajour Abbey and pillaging by the lord of Aubignon's men, all

Gordes, general view.

of which brought about the abbey's decline. It had only two monks in 1443 when the chapter of St.Saviour's Cathedral in Aix purchased it. It became State property during the Revolution and was then used as a farm until 1846 when it was bought back by the State.

In accordance with the Cistercian Rule, the **church architecture** is an example of extreme simplicity. There is a very plain central doorway on whose tympanum are carvings of the arms of the chapter of Aix cathedral. Inside, there is a long nave with three spans, two side aisles, a transept, a sanctuary, and four apsidal chapels with a flat chevet.

Adjacent to the church are the conventual buildings — cloisters, sacristy, calefactory, dorter, and refectory (15th Century). The refectory is particularly outstanding. Fine Gothic vaulting rests on attractively-decorated capitals and, in addition, tall windows flank a large rose window flooding the room with light.

General view of Silvacane Abbey.

The interior of Silvacane Church.

AVIGNON

(Vaucluse, 62 miles N-W. of Marseilles)

To visit Avignon is to step right into a living history lesson. It is said to be in this town that the poet Petrarch (1304-1374) first met the Laura whose praises he sang in his poetry. Today, it is the home of theatre for one month of the year (mid-July to mid-August) and to us, in Fulco de Baroncelli's words, it is « Delicious Avignon ».

The town really entered the pages of History with the installation of the papacy in France in the 14th Century. It was the atmosphere of insecurity in Rome and pressure from the King of France, Philip the Fair, which persuaded Bertrand de Got, Bishop of Bordeaux, to remain in France after his election as Pope in 1305 under the name Clement V. At the time the Popes, although lords of the nearby comtat Venaissin, did not own Avignon; it belonged to Charles II of Anjou, Count of Provence and vassal to the Pope through his position as King of Sicily. Clement V arrived in Avignon on 9th March 1309 and took up residence in the Dominican monastery, although he spent the summer months in the mountains of the comtat Venaissin. On his death in 1316, the former Bishop of Avignon, John XXII, was chosen as his successor and this detail was to be of vital importance for the town. The new Pope, who already knew and appreciated the episcopal palace, chose it as his main place of residence. From then onwards, although he had proclaimed his intention of returning to Rome, he remained in Avignon and, until his death on 4th December 1334, the papal court was established in the Bishop's Palace (which no longer exists) and the Dominican monastery. It was on the election of his successor, Benedict XII, that Avignon ceased to be merely a temporary residence and became the permanent seat of the papacy. This austere Pope, an avowed enemy of Luxury, undertook to rebuild the palace from top to bottom, and his creation known as

The St.Peter-and-St.Paul Gate in the Popes' Palace.

the « Old Palace », which resembles a citadel-monastery, forms a stark contrast to the adjacent luxurious « New Palace » built on the orders of the following Pope, Clement VI. He it was who also purchased the town of Avignon from Queen Jeanne. From then on, the Pope was truly at home in Avignon. The next three popes, all also of French extraction, made little impact on the palace whatever building work they may have ordered.

It was during the reigns of Innocent VI's two successors that Avignon ceased to be the ideal

« natural » place of residence for the Holy See, especially as it was often threatened by highwaymen. The poet Petrarch, a frequent visitor to the papal court, expressed in the most violent terms the feeling shared by the numerous people who were demanding the Pope's return to Rome. He had absolutely no hesitation in accusing the town of being an « impious Babylon, a cesspool of vice, and the sewer of the earth ». The first of the aforementioned successors, Urban V, kept Rome in mind, especially as the Italian provinces had settled down again and all the unrest had ceased

in the Eternal City. He decided to return in 1365 but was unable to leave Avignon until 1367. In 1370, he chose to come back, and he died here in December of that year. His successor, Gregory XI, again attempted to take the Holy See back to Rome, where he died on 27th March 1378. This time, it resulted in the great schism of the Western world, at a tragic period of history when four plague epidemics (in 1348, 1360, 1369, and 1375) killed millions of Christians. The new Pope, Urban VI, who was elected somewhat hastily, had a blundering and insulting attitude towards the cardinals. Indeed, things reached the point where thirteen French cardinals left Rome and, with the backing of King Charles V of France, elected an « anti-pope », Clement VII, on 20th September 1378. The Christian world then split into two camps, support for Clement VII coming from as far afield as the kingdoms of France, Scotland, Aragon, Castile, and Portugal, Cyprus, and the County of Savoy. Quite naturally, Clement VII and his court settled in Avignon in 1379. The last anti-pope, Benedict XIII, left Avignon in 1403 but it was not until 1429 that the

Top: *Mercury base in the Great Audience Chamber.*

Left: *the Pope's bedchamber in the Angel Tower.*

Bottom: *the upper gallery in the cloisters.*

The octagonal mitre in the kitchens of the Popes' Palace.

Right: *St.John's Chapel.*

last of his supporters submitted to Martin V, Pope of the entire Christian world, in the face of general indifference.

The **Papal Palace**, then, is really the work of two popes with very different temperaments, Benedict XII and Clement VI, who gave it its final appearance to all intents and purposes. The outside is impressive. Visitors are faced by a massive 15,000 m² fortress equipped with a frightening system of defence. Built directly on the rock, it is striking for the height of its square towers (some of them more than 160 ft.), its machicolations, its battlements, its slit windows and its Gothic arches. The French architects in charge of the work were Pierre Poisson, who was chosen by Benedict XII, then, from 1344 to 1358, Jean de Louvres who often showed considerable lack of skill. As to the main artists, they were Italian — Simone Martini, and Matteo di Giovanetti and his pupils. After Benedict XIII left the palace, it was never again occupied by a pope, although part of it was the residence of the papal legates. Their presence did not prevent the deterioration of a palace that was too old and that no longer served any useful purpose. The Revolution and the wars which turned it into barracks merely worsened what was often irreparable damage. The furniture was scattered, and the statues and sculptures were broken. It was not until after the First World War that restoration began.

The main entrance is the **Champeaux Gate** topped by defensive turrets. The vast **Consistory Chamber** (it measures 110 ft. by 34 ft.) lies in the eastern wing of Benedict XII's cloisters, in the Old Palace. Note the small door in the south wall through which the Cardinals entered. During consistories, the Council of Cardinals was summoned by the Pope. Unlike the meetings that take place today, these assemblies played a very precise and important rôle — they formed the sovereign Court and the Supreme Council of the Christian world. This is where the Pope formally welcomed visiting royalty; it was here that he announced the names of new Cardinals or that requests for canonisation were studied. In those days, the walls were covered with frescoes by Matteo di Giovanetti but they were destroyed during the great fire which destroyed all this part of the palace in 1413. They have now been replaced by some fine Gobelins tapestries and by historical documents. It was the fire that gave the eastern wall its pink tinge; adjacent to it is the **St. John Tower**, a small square tower with walls some 6 1/2 ft. thick.

It contains the two famous **chapels-St.John's** which is entered by one of the doors in the Consistory Chamber, and **St. Martial's** on the floor above. St. John's still has its original frescoes, the work of Clement VI's favourite artist, Matteo di Giovanetti. They depict scenes from the lives of the two St.Johns — St.John the Baptist (on the east and north walls) and St.John the Evangelist (on the south and west walls). The west wall, for example, shows the **Recommendation of the Virgin**

Mary to St. John during the Crucifixion. On the badly-damaged vaulting, one can just make out the figures of the first great saints.

Visitors then go up to the first floor where, above the Consistory, is one of the largest rooms in the palace (156 ft. long and 33 ft. wide) originally used for great ceremonial banquets. This is the « Grand Tinel » (from the latin word « tina » meaning « barrel ») containing frescoes by Simone Martini, an artist from Sienna. They come from the porch in the cathedral of Notre-Dame-des-Doms.

A door in St. John's tower leads into **St. Martial's Chapel** which still has the frescoes painted by Matteo di Giovanetti and his pupils in 1344-1345. Opposite the door is a **Crucifixion** scene; all the other frescoes depict the life and miracles performed by St. Martial. The choice of this follower of Christ from Limoges was doubtless the result of Clement VI's Limousin origins. The outstanding series of paintings has suffered a great deal of damage as is obvious from the large number of heads that have been removed. It is said that these fragments were sold by the soldiers billetted in the palace.

The Pontif's apartments between the « Palace Square » (or **Great Courtyard**) and the Orchard, date from the reign of Benedict XII, except for the **Wardrobe Tower** (1342). In the centre of the **Angels' Tower** built by Pierre Poisson (it was renamed in the 16th Century; in the 14th and 15th Centuries it was known as the Pope's Tower or the Great Tower) is the **Pope's bedroom**, a vast chamber that was once divided off into smaller rooms by mobile partitions. It has a fireplace in one corner and two large bay windows. Its decoration, distemper on a blue background, has been restored. It is a simple coat of paint over bare stone. Visitors will notice the red and grey foliage containing birds and squirrels. It is thought that this lively decorative pattern dates from the reign of Clement VI who wished to replace his predecessor's much more austere decoration.

The **Wardrobe Tower** was built at Clement VI's request. It housed a steam bath or bathroom, two storeys of dressing rooms, the **Hall of the Deer** and finally a private chapel. The Hall of the Deer, a much more intimate room than the Pope's bedroom, was his study as well as his rest room. The decoration is springlike, contrasting with the religious subjects chosen for other rooms. The various scenes, painted by an unknown artist, depict a landscape planted with all kinds of trees with slender trunks bearing flowers or fruit and with branches full of birds. There are a variety of subjects — fishing in a pool filled with a large number of fish, especially broach; bird and stag-hunting (hence the name given to the chamber); falconry; and children's games.

The palace that Clement VI took over from Benedict XII was closed off to the south by John XXII's Audience Chamber and, to the west, by private houses. Moreover, the main courtyard was too small to cater for the crowds who came seeking benedictions or indulgences on major occasions. The

Popes' Palace: a fresco in the Hall of the Deer.

The bust of Benedict XII by Paul of Sienna.

Pope had the idea of demolishing the offending buildings in order to extend the courtyard and re-erecting nobler buildings suitable for holding a more sumptuous **audience. During the building** work, Clement VI decided that he wanted an even more prestigious decor and that the walls of the audience chamber should be raised so that a chapel could be built over the top, a chapel that would be more spacious than the one built by Benedict XII. He inaugurated this **Great Chapel** (also known as Clement VI's Chapel) on All Saints' Day 1352. In order to build the Gothic nave, the architect, Jean de Louvres, had to cover the entire width of the Great Audience Hall (49 ft.) without exceeding the average height of the castle (hence the height of only 62 ft.). The doorway into the Great Chapel dedicated to St. Peter and St. Paul was originally richly decorated; today, of the four statues in the niches, only the one of St. Peter is left and it is in very poor condition. This is where the Cardinals of the Conclave (which assembles in absolute secrecy ten days after the Pope's death in order to elect a successor) used to attend the

Mass of the Holy Spirit. They then went back, by a narrow passage-way called the **Conclave Gallery** which has tiny crossed ogival arches, to the first storey of the Old Palace since the discussions and voting took place in St. Martial's Chapel. Opposite the main door of the chapel is the large **Indulgence Window** where the newly-elected Pope received the papal crown and where, at the end of the Mass, he gave his blessing or announced indulgences.

Next, visitors go up the wide straight **great staircase** leading to the hall in front of the chapel, and into the very beautiful **Great Audience Chamber** on the ground floor of the New Palace. This magnificent hall (169 ft. long, 51 ft. wide and 36 ft. high) was built in 1345. It is divided in two by five pillars, each flanked by eight colonettes bearing the springing of the ogival arches which, in their turn, rest on bases carved each with a different motif — a wild boar armed with a sword and shield, a winged dragon crouching down, a quadruped with the head of a monkey etc. In Clement VI's days, the Audience Chamber was especially famous for its frescoes (by Matteo di Giovanetti) of which, apart from the **Prophets Fresco** (1353), all that is left is unfortunately a few fragments and traces of drawings sketched on the walls. It was in this chamber, in the double east span to be precise, that the thirteen eccesiatical judges would sit when hearing major cases. The Audience Chamber was also known as the « Wheel Court » (tribunal de la Rote), doubtless because the judges sat in a circle, the Latin word « rota » meaning « a wheel ».

The Popes' Palace is now a major centre of culture and communication. The main courtyard of the palace is the setting for the best-known works presented during the **Theatre Festival** founded in 1946 by Jean Vilar, while the Conclave Wing has been restored and turned into a Conference Centre equipped with the most up-to-date audiovisual equipment.

The cathedral of Notre-Dame-des-Doms.

Left: *the walls of Avignon.*

The **Place du Palais** also has a number of interesting buildings. Visitors may care to admire, for example, the fine richly-carved 18th-century Baroque façade of the **Mint**, now the Academy of Music. It is decorated with cherubs, garlands of fruit, and, on the balustrade, with dragons and eagles, the emblems of the Cardinal Scipio Borghese.

Standing proudly above the esplanade is the **Cathedral of Notre-Dame-des-Doms**. The present church, built c.1150 on a site that had always been sacred, is the only Romanesque building in Avignon. Despite historical incidents and successive additions, it has maintained its original character and majestic simplicity. It is topped by a square belltower built c.1425 on which, since 1829, there has been an impressive statue of the Virgin Mary. In front of the tower is a Romanesque porch of Gallo-Roman inspiration which used to be decorated with frescoes by Simone Martini that have been in the Palais des Papes since 1962 —

the «**Virgin Mary surrounded by angels**» and «**Christ giving His benediction**». Inside is a single aisle to which side chapels were added between the 14th and 16th Centuries. Especially outstanding is the octagonal cupola and its small lantern tower above the transept crossing. At the entrance to the chancel is a white marble Bishop's Throne decorated on the sides with the lion of St. Mark and the ox of St. Luke. John XXII and Benedict XII were buried in Notre-Dame-des-Doms. The Flamboyant Gothic tomb of John XXII is in the chapel beside the sacristy while Benedict XII's tomb is in the apse. Unfortunately what one sees today is a 19th-century copy which bears little resemblance to the original.

From the nearby **Rocher des Doms** on which the town stood in prehistoric times, there is an uninterrupted panoramic view of the Rhône, the Saint-Bénezet Bridge,

John XXII's tomb in Notre-Dame-des-Doms.

and Villeneuve-lès-Avignon. At the end of the esplanade is the **Petit Palais** (the Small Palace, so-called to differentiate it from the Popes' Palace). Before becoming the archbishops' residence, it belonged to Cardinal Arnaud de Via, John XXII's nephew. It was rebuilt in the 15th Century. The façade, with its wide windows, is topped by battlements and was designed by Cardinal Julien de la Rovère (1475-1503). Several famous people stayed there, e.g. Caesar Borghia in 1498, François I in 1533, Anne of Austria and the Duke of Orleans in 1660. Nowadays, it houses an art gallery of some twenty rooms, its most important exhibits being the 300 Italian primitives in the Campana Collection. The famous work by Botticelli, «**Madonna and Child**», is particularly admirable.

Avignon's old districts are also worth a visit. The **Balance District** has been renovated and has both modern housing and fine restored mansions. To the south, **St. Peter's Church**, decorated with an admirable 14th-century tower and magnificently-carved Renaissance doors, is a good example of regional Gothic architecture. At the junction of the rue des Marchands and the rue des Fourbisseurs is the interesting **Rascas Residence**.

In the Dyers' Quarter, there are a number of fine mansions such as the **Berton de Crillon**, **Fortia de Montreal**, and **Honorati de Jonquerettes Residences**. Then there is the nearby **St. Didier's Church**, a masterpiece of Provençal Gothic architecture.

Another remarkable church stands in the **County Buildings District — St. Agricola's**. Not far away is the **Le Roure Palace**, once the home of a Florentine moneylender, which has a magnificent door decorated with carvings of intertwined branches. In the rue Joseph-Vernet, you will come to the beautiful and vast **Villeneuve-Martignan Residence** (18th Century), better-known as the **Calvet Museum**. It owes its name to the humanist doctor who lived in the Age of Enlightenment and bequeathed his art collections and his library to his home town.

It goes without saying that all visitors take a stroll on the **place de l'Horloge**. In Roman times, this was the forum. The outstanding features of this square planted with plane trees are the **theatre** and **town hall** (19th Century) flanking the **Clock Tower** (14th-15th Centuries) that is the last reminder of the Gothic period.

These days, especially when the Festival is in full swing, its many cafés draw large crowds come to watch numerous improvised entertainments.

Finally, before going to the Saint-Bénezet Bridge, you may like to take a walk near the **city walls** (they are almost 3 miles long), built during the reigns of Popes Innocent VI and Urban V. They are notable for the defects that make them useless from a military point of view — the towers are open on the town side and some of the walls lack machicolations. The ramparts were built in haste. They were then repaired and partially restored in the late 15th Century and again during the Wars of Religion. There was one final period of restoration in the 19th Century, under the management of Viollet-le-Duc.

The **Saint-Bénezet Bridge** dates from before the time of the popes in Avignon. A Provençal legend tells how it was built in 1177 by Bénezet, a young shepherd from the Vivarais Region, and opened to traffic in 1185. Before undertaking his task, he is said to have heard voices ordering him to build a bridge across the Rhône at a place specified by an angel. He succeeded in lifting very heavy stones without any effort at all and, when this « miracle » came to people's ears, gifts of money poured in and the bridge was built. It is now thought to be Roman in origin, Bénezet having taken part in its rebuilding. In any case, it is almost half-a-mile long and was the first bridge to cross the Rhône inland from the sea. It was quickly used by travellers and pilgrims come to see Bénezet's relics which were then

The Saint-Bénezet Bridge in Avignon.
Overleaf: *general view of Avignon.*
The clock tower in Avignon.

transferred to the town itself before disappearing during the Revolution. It fell victim to flooding on several occasions despite having been built with piers to improve its resistance, and it was rebuilt several times until, in the mid-17th Century, it was abandoned. It now has only four spans and rather strangely bears a Romanesque and Gothic chapel dedicated to St. Nicolas (the patron saint of sailors), the two shrines being one on top of the other. The bridge was, though, too narrow for people to dance on as the song would have it; it was beneath the arches of the bridge above Barthelasse Island that the people of Avignon used to make merry.

VILLENEUVE-LES-AVIGNON
(Vaucluse, 2 miles N. of Avignon)

From Villeneuve-lès-Avignon, situated in a very beautiful spot on the right bank of the Rhône, there is a famous, and truly lovely panoramic view over the « Pope's Town », especially at sunset. From time immemorial, man has recognised the advantages of this site. The prehistoric settlement on Mont Adaon (the original name of the Saint-André Hill which was an island until the branch of the Rhône was drained) was followed by a succession of places of worship — a Gallo-Roman altar, a Paleochristian hermitage, and finally a Benedictine abbey (10th Century) around which huddled the houses in the tiny village of Saint-André. Because of its strategic position, the Kingdom of France set out as far back as the first half of the 13th Century to acquire this rock overlooking the river, which was even more important inasmuch as it stood opposite the County of Provence and the proud town of Avignon. In 1292, Philip the Fair decided to build a « new town ». It was this period that saw the erection of Philip the Fair's Tower at the entrance to the Saint-Bénezet Bridge. In the following century, John the Good and Charles V built the Saint-André Fortress. The second piece of luck for the town was the establishment of the Holy See and papal Court in Avignon in the 14th Century; it became a residential suburb. Cardinals built exquisite town houses here, called « livrées ». It was to this that the community owed its most important building — **the Val-de-Bénédiction Carthusian monastery.** The town was to remain prosperous long after the departure of the Popes, indeed until the Revolution.

Built between 1293 and 1305, **Philip the Fair's Tower** originally had only one storey. It was the lar-

Left: *the Carthusian monastery in Villeneuve-lès-Avignon — the St.John cloisters.*
General view of the Carthusian monastery in Villeneuve-lès-Avignon.

gest section in a barbican guarding the entrance to the Saint-Bénezet Bridge and controlling traffic using it. A second storey was added in the 14th Century. There is a very fine view from the upper terrace over the whole surrounding area.

A walk around the **Saint-André Fortress** also provides visitors with a panoramic view of Avignon, the Lubéron and the Alpilles. This stronghold, dating from the second half of the 14th Century, is a magnificent example of mediaeval military architecture. The most impressive features are the size of the outer wall and the two massive towers flanking the fortified gateway; they originally served as a keep. Inside the fortress was the Romanesque **Chapel of Notre-Dame-de-Belzévet** (12th Century) and the **Benedictine Abbey of Saint-André** but only their ruins now remain.

A stroll through Villeneuve will take you to the parish church, once a collegiate church (1333) founded by Cardinal Arnaud de Via, and give you a chance to admire a 14th-century polychrome ivory statue of the Virgin Mary in the sacristy (15th Century). It was carved out of an elephant tusk.

The **Almshouse Municipal Museum** houses many masterpieces from the Carthusian monastery, the most notable being a splendid copy of a Pietà (the original is on show in the Louvre) and a « **Coronation of the Virgin Mary** » painted in 1453.

It is, though, **the Carthusian monastery of Val-de-Bénédiction** which is the real aim of any visit. The precise reasons for its creation are still unknown. There is a commonly-held belief that, on the death of Clement VI in 1352, the Prior of the Grande Chartreuse, dom Jean Birelle, was elected Pope but refused the office because of his humility. Cardinal Etienne Aubert was elected in his place. The story goes that as a sign of his gratitude the Cardinal, by then Pope Innocent VI, founded the monastery on 2nd June 1356. Yet what was originally no more than an ordinary

St. Andrew's Fort in Villeneuve-lès-Avignon.

town house destined to receive twelve fathers and a prior became, through the efforts of Innocent VI's two nephews, a quite exceptional monastery. The huge group of buildings, the largest Carthusian monastery in France, is protected by a wall more than half-a-mile long laid out around its three cloisters — the small church cloister, the great cloister in the cemetery surrounded by the fathers' cells, and the St.John cloister around which are the cells of the Carthusian

monks. Since the 14th Century there has been a well in the centre of its garth to which, in the 17th Century, a fountain topped by a statue of Christ was added while in the 18th Century a rotunda was erected. Although the edge of the well and the basin of the fountain are still there, the statue has unfortunately disappeared.

During the Revolution, the monastery lost most of its furniture. Nevertheless, it is possible to glean some idea of daily life there by visiting one of the Fathers' Houses which has been set out as in days gone by near the cemetery cloisters. In the church is **Innocent VI's tomb**, a veritable treasure of Gothic architecture.

UZÈS
(Gard, 15 miles N. of Nîmes)

The Uzès rock, standing in a landscape of scrub, justifiably gives an impression of peaceful preserva-tion from which the past reappears at every turn and in every stone. At its foot flow the tranquil waters of the R. Eure or Alzon.

Man occupied this site far back in his history and everything began in the valley, near the sources of the R. Eure. In Roman times, a highly-prosperous residential town develo-ped under the name *Ucetia* and, in the 4th Century, a bishopric was founded that was to last until 1790.

In the 11th Century, the town acquired the appearance that chan-ged very little until modern times. The first cathedral was built in 1090, and the first fortifications were erected in 1148. An important date in the town's history was 1229 when the County of Uzès was uni-ted with the Crown of France. Thenceforth, three people held power — his Lordship, the Bishop and the King. In 1346, the manor of

The Fenestrelle tower in Uzès.

Uzès: *the organ in St. Théodorit's Cathedral.*

Top right: *general view of Uzès*
Bottom right: *the arcades on the Place aux Herbes in Uzès.*

Uzès became a viscountcy, while in 1486 Symone, the Viscount's last heir, married Jacques Loys de Crussol. The de Crussols then found fame in high functions entrusted to them by the monarch. The 16th Century was deeply marked by the Reformation which in Uzès degenerated into a veritable war of religion that was to last until the end of the century. The Catholics became a minority and the members of the Reformed Religion demolished the cathedral in 1563. It was during this tragic period, in 1565, that the Viscountcy was raised to the position of « Premier Duchy in France ».

Despite the troubles, the town's material prosperity greatly increased over the 17th and 18th Centuries. Work on the new cathedral began in 1644 and was completed in 1663. Building started on the bishop's palace in 1671. It is impossible to talk about the 17th Century in Uzès without mentioning the 18-month stay by the great poet and playwright Jean Racine from November 1661 onwards; he lived with his maternal uncle, Canon Sconin. His « Letters from Uzès » to the Parisians contain a multitude of precious detail about day-to-day life in the town. One of them includes the famous sentence, « And we have nights that are more beautiful than your days ». In the 18th Century, private residences and a number of rich mansions were refurbished or built. The six towers along the ramparts were demolished, and the present town hall was built, as was **St.Stephen's Church**. Once the town's defences had been removed, the town became outward-looking and boulevards were built over the former moats, cool shady places for a stroll.

In the centre of the old town is the only castle in France to have the honour of bearing the name of **Duchy**. This large building (it is open to the public) has origins lost in the mists of time (the Gallo-Roman period) and it was already a fortress in the 11th Century. The oldest section is the **Viscountcy**, comprising one building and a tower (14th Century) and more importantly the **Bermonde Tower**, an 11th-century square keep whose summit was demolished during the Revolution and rebuilt in 1839. From its terrace, the eye travels aross the old town and the surrounding scrublands. The perfectly-preserved Renaissance façade was built to designs by Philibert Delorme. It shows one of the earliest examples of Classical superimposition — Doric, Ionic and Corinthian.

St. Théodorit's Cathedral, which is adjacent to the north wall of the **bishop's palace**, stands on an esplanade of horse chestnuts leading to a terrace from which there is a view over the valley and the surrounding heath. Built in the 17th Century, its present façade was rebuilt in the 19th. Inside, note the fine organ from the time of Louis XV. It is, though, the **Fenestrelle Tower** (12th Century) pierced with windows (hence its name, « fenestrelle » meaning just that) which is especially admirable. It stands on the right-hand side of the old cathedral. This is the only tangible reminder of the old Romanesque cathedral. It is 137 ft. high and comprises six circular storeys, each set slightly back from the preceding one. At the top is a round belltower. It is remarkable for its elegance and austerity.

You may also care to visit the **Bishop's Clock Tower** (12th Century) and **St. Stephen's Church** (18th Century). And it is very pleasant to stroll around the **place de la République** (formerly the place aux Herbes) on market day, or to admire the fine house fronts on the private mansions in **the rue Jacques-d'Uzès** or **the rue de la République**.

NIMES
(Gard, 19 miles N-W. of Arles)

Nîmes is a very busy town of many faces. Tourists will be attracted to the artistic town and its very fine Roman buildings. Yet it is also a large industrial and textile centre (which interested Italian merchants as far back as the 13th Century), and an important market place for wine. One of the town's charms is the narrowness of its streets, with the long terraces of yellow ochre houses bearing wrought-iron balconies. Some of them are of historical and artistic interest, although this is not generally known. There is a **Romanesque house** at No.1 rue de la Madeleine near the cathedral, decorated with carvings of animals, and a **Gothic house** at No.15 rue des Marchands. Finally, it should be remembered that the writer Alphonse Daudet was born on 13th May 1840 at No.20 boulevard Gambetta, into a family of scarfmakers. In his book, « The Little Weakling », he gives a description of his native town.

Long ago, in the Late Stone Age, man lived here near a gushing fresh water spring, now known as the « source de la Fontaine » at the foot of Mont Cavalier. Before being colonised by Rome, the town was the capital of the Volscians (the Celtic word means « the land of those who live in the plains ») who were a highly-civilised tribe. *Nemausus*, the Latin name for Nîmes, was long considered to be the name of a local god whom the Volscians honoured in this spring. In fact, it would seem that the name simply means « a spring » or that it is a reminder of a nearby sacred wood. In any case, the town was an important market that was well-served by its position on the road, and in 16 B.C. it became the « Colonia Augusta Nemausensis » without any undue problems. Emperor Augustus then founded a Roman town which attracted Roman colonials who had taken part in victorious campaigns in Egypt and along the Nile. This explains why the coat-of-arms of the town of seven hills, a verita-

Left: the Magne Tower in Nîmes.

Fragments of sarcophagi at no.6 rue de l'Aspic in Nîmes.

The Maison Carrée in Nîmes.

Right: *the Augustus Gate in Nîmes*

ble « French Rome », still includes a crocodile chained to a palm tree. During this period, mighty ramparts were built to protect a number of magnificent monuments. The town's prosperity reached its peak under the Antonines, in the 2nd Century A.D. It could then be considered as one of the largest towns in Gaul but it was to go into a rapid decline with the onset of the barbarian invasions (5th Century). First it was the Visigoths who drove out the Romans and settled there, mainly in the amphitheatre which they guarded by means of a moat and two towers. These partisans of the great Aryan heresy tried to impose it on the Catholic population, which had been converted by two missionaries in the 3rd Century — St. Saturnin and St. Baudille. They increased their persecution until the 8th Century, shutting down the churches. Then the Saracens drove the Visigoths out before Charles Martel put a stop to their advance. Nîmes came out of these difficult times badly scarred and with a greatly-diminished population. It was in the 11th Century that it began to develop again, after the Counts of Toulouse had taken possession of the town. It was at this time that St. Castor's Cathedral was consecrated (1096).

Religious strife reappeared with the Albigensian heresies of the 13th Century supported by Raimond VI, Count of Toulouse, among others. However, Simon de Montfort at the head of the Anti-Albigensian crusaders took Nîmes and made it the property of the kings of France. It then became a prosperous trading town and a major textile centre. Unfortunately religious conflict was soon to arise anew. In 1389, the Jews who had been an integral part of the Nîmes community since the 7th Century without any difficulty, had their property confiscated and were driven out of the town. In 1532, Nîmes was affected by the Reformation and in 1562 the so-called « religionaries » became the masters of the town. It was in 1566 that the most terrible event took place — on the evening of St. Michael's Day, there was a riot (since known as the « Michelade ») during which the main churches were ransacked and

one hundred Catholics tortured in the courtyard of the bishop' palace. From 1570 onwards, the town was little influenced by the religious struggles taking place elsewhere; indeed, it provided an example of peaceful coexistence between the two communities. It took advantage of this to develop and it was this period that saw the building of elegant mansions belonging to the tradesmen of Nîmes, the 18th-century town hall, and the great Protestant church built between 1714 and 1747. The last tragic event was the « White Terror » fomented by Trestaillons and Truphémy which had particularly violent repercussions here. Yet economic activity continued to develop, marked in the 19th Century by the arrival of the railway and the widescale industrial development of the entire region.

A visit to Nîmes might well begin with the most famous monument in Roman Gaul — the **Maison Carrée**, or Square House, which is in fact a rectangle 85 ft. long, 49 ft. wide, and 55 ft. high. This temple, the best-preserved of its kind anywhere in the Roman world, shows

very clear indications of the Greek influence. Its pure lines stand above a monumental base 9 ft. high and in Roman times it was surrounded by a portico with carved pillars. The perfection of the carvings on the Corinthian capitals along the frieze and cornice is admirable; they consist of a double row of acanthus leaves. Like many of the monuments in Nîmes, the date of its construction long posed a problem. However, thanks to research by the local archaeologist J-F. Poirier in the 18th Century, we now know that the shrine was dedicated to Augustus' two grandsons, Caius and Lucius Caesar, who had been adopted by the emperor in the hope that one of them would be his successor. Alas, they died a premature death in the years 2 and 4 A.D. It is, then, possible to date the Maison Carrée from the period between their adoption in 12 B.C. and the beginning of the Christian era. Over the centuries, the Maison Carrée has been used as an assembly hall, a town hall, and an Augustinian convent after having narrowly missed being taken to Versailles in the 17th Century. Colbert wanted to dismantle it and re-erect it in the park there!

Today it is the **Museum of Antiquities**, housing some very interesting fragments of local ancient monuments — mosaics, bas-reliefs, pillars, and statues including a gigantic one of Apollo, a white marble head of Venus and a bronze head of Apollo. One of the most noteworthy exhibits is without doubt the **Eagle frieze** which came from a long-gone building in Nîmes, the Plotine Basilica built in the reign of Emperor Hadrian in honour of his adoptive stepmother, Trajan's wife.

Another museum worth a visit is the **Museum of Archaeology** in the former Jesuit College. On the ground floor are numerous pieces of sculpture, while on the first floor there is a room showing day-to-day life in Gallo-Roman times. In the last room is the former medallion from the Maison Carrée.

Standing proudly in the centre of the town, the **amphitheatre** is the best example of Nemausus' glorious past. It was here that three types of entertainment took place — fights (against bulls, wild boar or bears), athletic competitions, and gladiatorial combat. They were held at the hottest time of day and a « velum », a sort of awning, was strung above the spectators to provide them with shade. The amphitheatre is similar to the one in Arles as regards size and layout, only differing by the shape of the arches which in this case are cradle-vaults. Dating probably from the 1st Century A.D., and although it only ranks twentieth on the list of amphitheatres, it is undoubtedly the best-preserved. It can still cater for 16,000 people in the 34 rows of stone seats within the ellipse measuring 432 ft. by 328 ft.

From the outside the regular and rather heavy style of the building may give it an overpowering appearance. The only rhythms for the eye to follow are the one hundred and twenty open arches (one above the other on two storeys, each one 68 ft. in height) and the dark pillars. The ground floor is decorated with pilasters. On the north wall is a rectangular pediment marking the main entrance. Two foreparts in the shape of bulls project from the walls. There is also a gladiatorial contest and, on one of the pillars on the lower level, a bas-relief of the she-wolf of the Capitol.

The amphitheatre was occupied by the Visigoths in the 5th Century and turned into a fortress, then guarded by the knights of the amphitheatre before being taken over in the Middle Ages by the poor who built a village for 2,000 people within its walls. In the 19th Century, it was emptied and restored. Nowadays, during the *feria* at Whitsun, the amphitheatre comes alive. From the Friday to the Monday (and this since 1863) bullfight follows bullfight in the presence of a huge crowd. There are three different types of fight — the complete bullfight similar to the Spanish corrida, the provençal « fight » during which men whisk cockades from off the bulls which are finally slaughtered, and lastly the « capea » in which there is no killing.

On the summit of Mont Cavalier stands the **Magne Tower**, a famous polygonal enigma of stone and moss. Nobody knows whether this Roman building was part of fortifications, a watchtower, or a triumphal monument. The total lack of knowledge as to its age (was it built in the 1st Century B.C.?) only serves to deepen the mystery. Niches are visible in the lower section, then there is a plain storey topped by another storey decorated with pillars. Over the centuries, the tower has lost 32 ft.; today, it is 98 ft. high. As soon as it is mentioned, it calls to mind the gold-digger named Traucat who, in 1601 during Henri IV's reign, began to dig in the base of the tower in search of the fabulous treasure said to be buried there. However, he only succeeded in making the tower unstable and he was obliged to give up his search.

During the imperial era of Roman domination, the **Fountain Gardens** were the main place for enjoying one's leisuretime. It is quite likely that the fountain stood in the middle of Roman baths. Be that as it may, the most outstanding feature from the days of Antiquity remains the mysterious vaulted chamber known as the **Temple of Diana**, although there is no tangible link between this building and any religious cult. Despite the fire in 1576, it still has a large number of elements from a decoration that was both magnificent and abundant, suggesting that this was a sumptuous mansion or a library.

Other buildings used to ornament the Fountain Gardens. The existence of a **nymphea** (a sort of decorative pond) and especially of a small **theatre** uncovered in 1854 would suggest that this was a veritable leisure centre. The small theatre is the same size as an ancient Greek concert hall. It is supposed that, from its nine rows of stone steps, the locals could see shows given by

The amphitheatre in Nîmes.

a company of Greek artistes who came in the 2nd Century in order to revitalise the idea of Greek games. There also remains a swimming pool and a double-staircase leading to the spring.

In the 18th Century an ambitious project was set in motion with the aim of bringing the Roman gardens back to life. To be more precise, it was in Louis XV's reign that the miltary architect Maréchal undertook the work. Today only half the project is there for all to see and admire; it had to be abandoned because of the vast sums of money involved. The gardens were laid out with basins into which flows the water from the spring which is then taken to the main piece of ornamentation, the **nymphea**, a copy of the one built in the days of Ancient Rome.

Two other reminders of the Roman era merit a mention — firstly, the **castellum divisorium**, a sort of large water tower filled by the water collected near Uzès by the Pont du Gard aquaduc. It was uncovered in the 19th Century in a street in the north of Nîmes, the rue de la Lampèze. From there, ten dif-

Aerial view of the Pont-du-Gard.

erent sets of pipes led to the various districts, carrying 20,000 m³ of water per day. The other Roman building is the **Augustus Gate**, unfortunately partly in ruins, a section of the town walls built c.15 B.C. It has two arches reserved for chariots and, to each side, two narrow passageways for pedestrians.

In the old town of Nîmes, **Notre-Dame Cathedral** is worth a visit. It was dedicated to St. Castor. It dates from 1096 but underwent a series of alterations over the centuries and was almost entirely rebuilt in the 19th Century. On the façade is a fresco depicting scenes from the Old Testament.

Usually, a trip to Nîmes ends with a visit to the other museums in the town — the **Old Nîmes Museum**, or the **Art Gallery** which is one of the finest museums of folklore in France.

PONT-DU-GARD
(Gard, 16 miles N. of Nîmes)

It was on the orders of Augustus' son-in-law, Agrippa, that this marvel of Antiquity was built c.19 B.C., and it has remained almost intact right up until the present day. The bridge crosses the Gardon Valley and is the most spectacular section of an aquaduct almost 32 miles long. In the days of the Roman Occupation, it carried almost

The keep in Beaucaire castle.

20,000 m³ of water per day from the sources of the rivers Eure and Ayran near Uzès down to Nîmes.

A few figures serve to emphasise the Romans' technical achievement. The bridge is 159 ft. high, its width varies between 10 and 20 ft., and its maximum length is 894 ft! To build it, blocks of stone weighing several tons were hoisted up to a height of more than 130 ft.

The bridge is also a beautiful piece of work. Time has coloured the stone, giving it a golden hue that is even more attractive at sunset. The orderliness of the three rows of arches, each one set slightly back from the one below, is admir-able. Note, too, that each row of arches has its own particular dimension.

BEAUCAIRE
(Gard, 16 miles E. of Nîmes)

The pride of the town that rivals Tarascon, from which it is separated only by a bridge, is based on its past as a trading centre. The site first of a Roman encampment called Urgenum, then the mediaeval capital of the « Argence Region » belonging to the Viscounts of Narbonne and later to the Counts of Toulouse, it became the setting in 1217 for the « Madgalene Fair », officially founded by Raimond VI.

It was famous throughout Europe from the 13th to the 19th Century, attracting almost 100,000 visitors. It lasted for a week from 22nd to 28th July.

It was originally held on the banks of the Rhône, in front of the boats tied up along the bank that had come from every possible geographical location. There, customers and loungers alike came to buy sugar, cocoa, coffee, spices, tropical fruit etc. Later, the fair spread throughout the town, each street and district specialising in one particular form of trade. There was the rue des Bijoutiers (Jewellers' Street), the rue du Beaujolais, he rue des Marseillais (selling oil and soap), streets where traders sold cloth and canvas etc. A huge fairground was also laid out.

Commerce, though, was not the only attraction. Large numbers of jugglers, acrobats, comedians, and animal-tamers brought life to the streets and took advantage of the fair to work up their latest acts. Unfortunately, the arrival of the first trains in Beaucaire brought about the rapid decline of the fair to which the great Provençal poet Mistral has dedicated one complete song in his «Poème du Rhône».

Nowadays visitors can go in search of the attractive houses that are reminders of this past hustle and bustle, all of them between the Rhône and the Sète Canal. They can also visit the castle built by St. Louis and dismantled by Richelieu. All that remains untouched is the keep from which there is a fine view of the Rhône, Tarascon, and the surrounding countryside.

TARASCON
(Bouches-du-Rhône, 11 miles N. of Arles)

The name of this small town on the borders of an important early vegetable area immediately conjures up memories of a legendary monster, the Tarasque, and the hero of three novels by Alphonse Daudet, Tartarin. Tarascon, though, has other items of interest for tourists, starting with its magnificent castle.

Originally, **Tarascon** was an island in the middle of the Rhône known as Jernica which the Greeks turned into a trading post dependent on Marseilles. The accumulation of alluvial soil in the Rhône valley finally connected it to the left bank. When the Romans captured it, they built an entrenchment linking Spain and Italy, and they called it Tarusco from the name of the dragon who was said to frequent this marshland. So the Tarasque was born. Provençal tradition has is that a monster with a lion's head, six legs and a serpent's tail regularly emerges from the Rhône and

Overleaf: the castle seen from the tower of St. Martha's.

St. Martha's and Tarascon seen from the castle.

devours any children, adults and animals in its path. It took the arrival of Martha, Mary Magdalene's sister, whose relics are kept in the Romanesque church, to get the better of this terrible beast. The saint went to the holy wood at Nerluc where it used to hide, wrapped her belt round the monster which had been paralysed at the sight of the Cross, forced it to go round the town walls three times, and locked it away beneath the present castle built on the site of the old Roman encampment. Numerous carvings and paintings keep this legend alive, as does the Feast of the Tarasque when a procession is organised and a huge cardboard dragon is carried through the town on the feastday of St. Martha and at Whitsun. And woe betide the careless who get too near it — the carnival monster soon knocks them to the ground! It was King René who organised the first carnival in 1474 and who created the Order of the Knights of the Tarasque.

Standing opposite the fortress in Beaucaire, some of the walls of the famous castle with its massive silhouette are 156 ft. high and, thanks to its exceptional condition, we can see what a Gothic stronghold was like. Building began in the 12th Century and continued until the end of the 15th Century, under King René who divided his time between Aix and Tarascon. It became a prison from the 16th Century onwards and remained in use until 1926. Now it is open to the public; the moat has been refilled with water and the adjacent buildings have been demolished. It comprises a low courtyard with walls flanked by rectangular towers, and the main building protected by round or rectangular towers. The Flamboyant Gothic main courtyard does not have the strict austere appearance of the outside of the building; it shows marked elegance. Particularly admirable are the carved façades with their fine windows and a graceful winding staircase leading to the private apartments. Note, too, in the courtyard the niche containing the busts of King René and his wife, Joan of Laval. The prisoners were held in the **Clock Tower**. On the walls are the drawings they etched to wile away the time.

There are other buildings worth a visit e.g. the **town hall** housing «Souleiado» material and a splendid collection of wooden patterns used in their manufacture, or the **rue des Halles** and its 15th-century houses with arcades. **St. Martha's Church** is also notable. It stands near the castle and was founded in the 10th Century but rebuilt during the 12th when the saint's body was rediscovered. The crypt contains her carved sarcophagus (3rd-4th Century).

The Gothic courtyard in Tarascon castle.

Right: *Tarascon town hall.*

cloître des Cordeliers

THE ABBEY OF SAINT-MICHEL-DE-FRIGOLET

(Bouches-du-Rhône, 10 miles E. of Avignon)

Saint-Michel-de-Frigolet? Think of the « Letters from My Mill »; it was here that Daudet placed one of his truculent characters, Father Gaucher, and his rosary of olive stones. It was this same debonair monk who so greedily praised the virtues of Aunt Bégon's elixir, you know, « that green, golden, warm, sparkling, exquisite liqueur which lets the sun into your stomach ».

Lost amid the hills, in a paradise for strongly-scented herbs, lavender, olive trees, and cypress, the abbey's origins go back to the 10th Century. At that time, the monks in Montmajour founded a priory comprising the Romanesque St. Michael's Church which still exists, though it has been restored, with its attractive stone roof and cloisters (early 12th Century). Unlike Aix, Arles, or Montmajour, the carvings decorating Frigolet are less excessive because of its lack of colonettes.

After the Revolution, the monastery was used to house a college frequented by the young Frédéric Mistral. If his « Memoirs » can be believed, it was among these craggy slopes that his poetic temperament was forged. In 1858, the abbey was purchased by the Premonstratensians or White Canons who have remained there right up until the present day despite expulsions in 1880, 1903 and 1914-1918. Father Edmond, a mediaeval specialist, was to build fortifications and the **Church of the Immaculate Conception** with its overwhelming decoration.

The Church includes the **Chapel of Our-Lady-of-the-Right-Remedy** (11th Century) who is still the object of a very precise cult — women come there to pray for a son. Anne of Austria, whose wish was granted in 1638 when she gave birth to the future Louis XIV, donated some very fine woodpanelling surrounding fourteen paintings by Mignard.

The chapel of Notre-Dame-du-Bon-Remède.

SAINT-REMY-DE-PROVENCE

(Bouches-du-Rhône, 14 miles N-E. of Arles)

Saint-Rémy is spread out opposite the dazzling chain of the Alpilles, in the centre of the alluvial plain stretching between the Rhône and the Durance. This being so, the small well-preserved town surrounded by its walls is situated in an area of widescale fruit and market gardening. It produces and sells flower and vegetable seeds. Yet it is its large number of Roman remains which attract so many tourists. It was here that Michel de Nostradame, known as Nostradamus (1503-1566), was born in what is now called the Rue Hoche where his birthplace can still be seen, though in a very poor state of repair.

Glanum and the Antiquities:

A mile from the centre of Saint-Rémy, in a small valley and a grandiose landscape of rocky scarp slopes where the Alpilles have carved out a breach, **Glanum** offers visitors its astonishingly rich collection of archaeological remains. It was thought that a missing town called Glanon, whose erstwhile existence had been proved by texts and a Greek inscription, was to be found there. The digs undertaken in 1921 and which are still going on today proved this supposition to be true.

Glanon then played a vital strategic and commercial rôle. The presence of a spring explains the decision to build here, and the fact that it flows on an arid plateau made it all the more precious. It was worshipped as far back as the 6th Century B.C. — a nymphea and a shrine in honour of the little god Glan, or Glanis, were built nearby. A Greek-style town then developed, with its public and religious buildings, its baths, its fine mansions and less grandiose accommodation for travellers and pilgrims. Unfortunately, Glanon suffered several upheavals, especially c.102 B.C. Roman legionaries rebuilt it from 49 B.C. onwards and the town, thereafter called Glanum, reached its heyday in the 1st and 2nd Centuries A.D. For a long time it was thought that the town had been destroyed by the Barbarians but it now seems more likely that it was abandoned as from 270 A.D. because of lack of space and an already spiralling taxation system! The inhabitants settled instead in the fertile plains. This was how Saint-Rémy came into being.

It is preferable to enter Glanum from the north. It is there that, to each side of the great paved central thoroughfare, stand colonnades, fountains, and the rich mosaics of houses and baths that were modified several times. Note the **small basin in the House of Epona** (2nd century B.C.) and the Greek-style **House of the Antes** which underwent alteration during the Gallo-Roman period. A little further on are **Cybele's shrine** containing the small stele to Loreia, and the **house of Atys,** in which it is easy to ima-

Left: *the ruins of Glanum, the Epona house.*

The ruins of Glanum - columns.

gine the faithful seated on the great stone benches, come together to honour their gods or to take advantage of the cool evening air.

The **baths** date from the time of Julius Caesar and still contain the hot, cold, and warm rooms, and the hot bath. Next to them is a swimming pool and a **unctorium** where massage and beauty treatment were dispensed. In this room, a beautiful mosaic, perhaps the oldest mosaic in Gaul, shows four dolphins playing around a fishing net against a background of stylised waves. Beneath the paving stones in the main street is a pipe that was no doubt the old sewer.

In the centre of Glanum, within the vast rectangular forum with its covered galleries onto which backs a basilica, the noisy colourful crowd would attend public meetings, go shopping in the nearby market or stroll beneath the porticos. The two temples built one after the other with a peribolos (a three-sided precinct) were the setting for great religious assemblies in honour of Gallic, Greek, Roman, and Oriental gods respectively, and even of Augustus, Livy and Octa-

vius during the days of the Roman Empire.

Finally there is the oldest district, containing the **Sanctuaries**. Nor should one forget the **nymphea**, a basin indicating the site of a sacred spring; it was restored in 20 B.C. by Agrippa.

Of course, the digs have not finished in Glanum and the town has more than one surprise left up its sleeve.

Not far from Glanum are two Roman monuments dating from the 1st Century, the « **Antiquities** », now still miraculously erect after two thousand years, the most prestigious symbols of Saint-Rémy.

The **municipal arch** was the largest gateway into Glanum and the great road leading to the town passed beneath its single arch. Despite damage, it is a very successful piece of artistry and one of the oldest arches from Roman times. Despite their thickness (18 ft.), its east-and west-facing sides preserve a sense of lightness thanks to the frame of slim columns and the wealth of Greek-style decorations. On each side of the opening are statues of captives.

The **mausoleum of the Princes of Youth** is really a cenotaph, i.e. a monument erected in honour of a dead man but which does not contain his body. The very elegant lantern of the deceased, the best-preserved of all those from the days of Ancient Rome, is 59 ft. high and is decorated in a fashion that is both Greek and Roman. The monument still holds many a secret. Why was it built on this particular spot? For whom was it built? Long considered to be the tomb of rich people of note, H. Rolland believes it to be a cenotaph in memory of Augustus' grandsons who died a premature death. Be that as it may, the mausoleum's designers wanted to create a hymn to youth for, despite the funereal character of the monument, it is rather more concerned to celebrate life, courage and youth. You only have to look at the carved panels on each side of the great base — triumph over the Amazons, victorious horsemen, the massacre of the children of Niobe, and a duel for possession of Patroclus' body. The upper section has four openings and the second comprises a small circular temple. All that is

Right: *close-up of the municipal arch in Les Antiques.*

The Antiques: *the Jules mausoleum and the municipal arch.*

missing is the pine-cone which used to top the dome. It is young men, too, draped in their togas, who are depicted inside the cupola, beneath the attractive fish-scale stone dome.

Other sights:

Saint-Rémy does not seem to have suffered too badly from successive invasions by the Visigoths, Burgundians and, finally, the Saracens. In 1331, its first collegiate church began to take shape; all that remains today is the belltower which has been rebuilt since that time and which now stands over the large St. Martin's Church (19th Century). In the 14th Century, the community surrounded itself with walls while the 15th and 16th Centuries were the age of the fine mansions and aristocratic residences that can still be admired in the old streets of the town. Around the **town hall**, especially on the place **Favier**, the decor is decidedly Renaissance. It is worthwhile visiting the **Hôtel de Sade** (containing the very important finds from the archaeological digs) and the **Alpilles Museum**, which is unjustly little-known and which is housed in the vast Mistral de Montdragon residence. Visitors should also remember the famous **Cardinal's Tower** 2 miles away, well hidden in the depths of the countryside.

Finally, not far from the plateau that forms the backcloth for the Antiquities, is the old **monastery of Saint-Paul-de-Mausole** (late 12th Century), now a hospital. The eye is immediately drawn to the church tower, an amazing lantern-tower. The monastery also still contains its canonial cloisters, one of the masterpieces of Provençal Romanesque architecture. From beneath the shade of its arches, you can admire the finesse of the colonettes and the variety of carved capitals bearing foliage and small figures.

The painter Vincent Van Gogh received treatment here for a year from 8th May 1889 to 6th May 1890, during which time he completed many canvases using motifs that he found in the garden or could see from his bedroom window. He also painted portraits including one of the hospital warden and the famous « Self-portrait with a palette ».

Around the Alpilles:

It would take more than just a few days to get to know the Alpilles properly; their highest point is Les Opiès at 1,602 ft. From a distance, the ragged peaks make them look like real mountains. Before setting

The cloisters in Saint-Paul-de-Mausole in Saint-Rémy.

The ruined citadel in Les Baux.

Overleaf: *general view of Les Baux.*

The village of Les Baux.

off to conquer the Mont Blanc, Tartarin, Alphonse Daudet's hero, trained on the slopes of these « miniature Alps ». The 6,810-hectare forest alone covers one-third of the area of this vast limestone range formed during the era of Pyrenean folding. Geological finds, flora and fauna are all surprisingly rich here. There are a large number of drives possible from Saint-Rémy. This is an opportunity to discover, among other things, **Les Baux-de-Provence**, **Fontvieille**, its windmills and memories of Daudet, or the **Maillane** of Frédéric Mistral.

LES BAUX-DE-PROVENCE
(Bouches-du-Rhône, 12 miles N-E. of Arles)

The rocky landscape of Les Baux gives some idea of the upheavals that led to its creation. As is the case for all the mountains in limestone Provence, it was the dual thrust of the Alps and the Pyrenees that produced the Alpilles Range. The Baux plateau to the south, a mass of rock with fantastic shapes carved out by erosion, towers over the whole region, right down to the Mediterranean. Around Maillane, the road follows the rockfalls of the **Val d'Enfer** (Valley of Hell) which may have provided the Italian poet Dante with inspiration for the first songs in his « Divine Comedy ». In the 19th Century, Les Baux revealed bauxite to the world; it is the basis of modern aluminium production.

What, though, lies behind the proud ruins of the village and castle of Les Baux standing on this arid rock? The discovery of flint blades, polished stone axes and bone punches in the **Grotte aux Fées** (Fairy Grotto) proved that the site was already inhabited 2,000 years B.C. The caves that provided shel-

71

ter for the people of that time were to become stone quarries, which explains some of the geometrical shapes. The « **cathédrale d'images** » (Picture Cathedral) in particular is open to the public.

Yet the glory of Les Baux dates from the Middle Ages. In the late 10th Century, a castle was built on the rocky escarpment; this was the birth of the Les Baux family. The poet Mistral honoured it in the following terms, « The most eminent of all the great Provençal families by its age and its splendour, a race of eagles, vassal to no man ». In order to better emphasise their power, the lords of Les Baux were to affirm that they were descended from Balthazar, one of the Magi, and they then included the star of the Nativity in their coat-of-arms. Les Baux took as its motto, « A l'azar, Bautezar » (« By chance, Balthazar »). Gradually, they amassed land and honours until, if tradition is to be believed, they owned 79 fiefs in Provence. And it is true that their power extended to the Dauphiné and the comtat Venaissin. Moreover their attitude was ever one of rebellion and they opposed the Catalonian Counts in the struggle for authority over the County of Provence.

Yet Les Baux went through a period of peace in the 12th Century. Its fame throughout feudal Europe was linked to that of the troubadours. These poets, musicians and singers were often aristocrats. They brought a touch of gentleness and love to a world of violence through their courtly poetry and songs. They gathered round beautiful ladies when the « Courts of Love » were in session. These were meetings at which questions of chivalry and gallantry were debated. They also provided an occasion to give prizes for Provençal poetry. All the texts provide an elevated and refined picture of love. When a knight seeks perfection and

Top: *Queen Jeanne's pavilion in Les Baux-de-Provence.*

Bottom: *the dovecot in Les Baux-de-Provence.*

The Eyguière Gate in Les Baux-de-Provence.

Les Baux-de-Provence: *the Porce-let Mansion.*

Les Baux-de-Provence: *the window of a house.*

Les Baux-de-Provence: *the White Penitents' Chapel.*

Les Baux-de-Provence: *the Church of St. Vincent.*

faces a thousand dangers, it is all in an effort to prove his love for his lady. It is only after numerous feats that the lord will have his patience and virtue rewarded. The best-known of the troubadours who visited Les Baux are Pierre Vidal, Fouquet de Marseille, Gui de Cavaillon and Raimbaut de Vacqueiras.

On the death of Alix, the last princess of Les Baux, the village became part of the County of Provence and René of Anjou, the « Good King René » who inherited it, gave it to his wife Joan of Laval who enjoyed coming here for a rest. Les Baux were then made into a mere baronny annexed to the Crown of France, as was the rest of Provence. It was used as a reward for faithful servants of the kingdom. However, won over by the Protestant Reformation and hostile to Cardinal Richelieu, the town disappeared in 1632 on the orders of Louis XIII who made its inhabi-

tants demolish it with their own hands.

It was a dead town for almost three centuries; Les Baux were only

recently rediscovered by touris from all over the world.

Usually, you enter the village (Les Baux by the **Rue Porte-Ma**

Les Baux-de-Provence: *general view of the north-west.*

which was laid out during the last century. Visitors previously used the **Eyguières** or Water Gate. It is still visible today; in days gone by it enabled the inhabitants to pass from the village to the **Fountain Valley** where the parish church stood. Now there is a summer house there built for Jeanne de Quinqueran, Baroness of Les Baux in 1581. This Renaissance masterpiece, wrongly called « Queen Jeanne's pavilion », was to please the poet Frédéric Mistral so much that he had a copy of it made for his grave in Maillane.

As you go towards the heart of Les Baux, you will pass the fine Renaissance façade of the **Porcelets' Mansion**. In the chamber on the ground floor, the vaulting has 18th-century frescoes depicting allegories of the four seasons. Next comes the Place Saint-Vincent. From the terrace, there is a superb panoramic view over the Valley of Hell. Two fine buildings add to the charm of this spot — the **White Penitents' Chapel** (17th Century) and **St.Vincent's Church**, undoubtedly founded in the 10th Century, rebuilt in the 12th Century, and topped by a tower that is a « lantern of the deceased », a square tower with rounded windows. Legend has it that a lamp was lit there, a reminder of the eternal light in the chancel of churches, every time somebody died. During the midnight Mass at Christmas, there is the festival of the shepherds which attracts large crowds. Shepherds in Provençal dress bring gifts of baskets of fruit and a new-born lamb placed in a tiny cart pulled by a ram.

The **Manville Mansion**, which proves how prosperous the town was in the 16th Century, has a Renaissance façade and a remarkable porticoed courtyard. It now houses the town hall and the Museum of Modern Art.

A protestant church was set up in an annex of this mansion at a time when the reformed religion was gaining a foothold in the town. All that remains of it now are ruins and, on the lintel of one of the windows is the Protestants' motto, « Post tenebra, lux » (« After the darkness, the light »).

The Rue Trencat dug out of the rock itself leads to the site of the old castle of which little was left after it had been demolished in the 17th Century. There is the **Paravelle Tower** which, with the Saracen Tower, was part of the inner defensive wall, the high ogival vaulting of the lower chamber, and the keep (13th Century) at the very top of the rock from which there is a magnificent view over the surrounding area. The remains of **St. Catherine's Church** are also interesting, as is an old stone dovecot (a « **colombarium** »). At the edge of the plateau stands a **monument** in honour of the Provençal poet **Charloun Rieu** (1848-1924), facing La Crau, the Vaccarès Lake, and the sea.

MONTMAJOUR ABBEY

(Bouches-du-Rhône, 3 miles N-E. of Arles)

As the only rock once jutting out from a huge stretch of marshland, the site of Montmajour Abbey, which had to be reached by boat, was always a sacred place. Long before monks settled there in the 10th Century, it had been a Christian graveyard.

It is said that St. Trophime, Bishop of Arles, sought refuge here in the 1st Century A.D. in order to escape persecution by the Romans. It is also said that Clovis' son gave the monks who had settled here a new church. Finally, Charlemagne is said to have fought the Saracens on this spot — and to prove it, graves were discovered containing the bodies of Christians who had died in battle.

In fact, it was not until 949 A.D. that the abbey was really established thanks to a gift from a woman called Teucinde. The monastery underwent rapid development. The Cistercian monks began to drain the surrounding marshes and, in order to finance this work, they created a well-known pilgrimage which attracted up to 150,000 believers. The abbey's fame increased still further when the first Counts of Provence asked to be buried here.

The decline of the monastery began in the 17th Century. At this time, both the Popes and the Kings of France entrusted its management to lay brothers who acquired an enormous income from their charge, without showing any exemplary faith. The Maurists settled here in 1639, succeeded in re-establishing discipline, and undertook the construction of new buildings in 1703; they were severely damaged by fire in 1726 and partially replaced. Its last Abbot, Cardinal de Rohan, having been implicated in the Queen's Necklace Affair, King Louis XVI had the abbey shut down in 1786 as a punishment. In 1791, it was sold as State property. Unfortunately two successive purchasers hastened to ransack it. Elisabeth Roux, a bankrupt, emptied it of all its splendours (books, marble, wood panelling and furnishings) before it was seized. The abbey was then sold again, this time to a property dealer who cut up the fine stone and sold off certain sections. In the 19th Century, the building was recovered and restored by Jacques Réattu and Pierre Révoil. The restoration work on what is again State property was completed only recently.

Tourists get the most attractive view of this mutilated architectural treasure as they drive up from **Fontvieille**. There is a fine panoramic view of the Alpilles, La Crau, Arles, the Cévennes ridge, Beaucaire and Tarascon from the upper platform in **Father Pons de l'Orme's Tower**. A scant two hundred yards from the abbey is the **Chapel of the Holy Cross** built in the shape of a Greek cross (late 12th Century). It stands amidst graves dug into the rock.

The keep in Montmajour Abbey.

The cloisters in Montmajour Abbey.

Montmajour: *the Holy Cross Chapel.*

All that remains of the accommodation, apart from the tower, are the chapter house and refectory above which used to be the dorter. The real masterpiece in the abbey is Notre-Dame Church (12th Century), a massive building with a very plain exterior. It comprises an unfinished upper church and a crypt partially dug into the rock. A door on the right-hand side at the end of the nave leads into the crypt. The cloisters, too, are remarkable. They were built in the second half of the 12th and the beginning of the 13th Century, while the southern gallery was not completed until the 14th Century. The galleries in the cloisters, which have a vaulted roof over arcades, are of varying degrees of interest. The north gallery, the oldest of the four, underwent complete restoration in the 19th Century whereas the west gallery was rebuilt in the 18th Century. The south gallery is Gothic in origin. Its carved capitals are richly decorated. The passage on the east side is the only remaining Romanesque gallery and it still has some fine capitals, all with floral motifs except for the splendid « **Temptation of Christ** ».

Daudet's windmill in Fontvieille

St.Peter's Chapel is also still standing, although it is not open to the public. It was the monastery's original church. Carved out of the south wall of the rock, it was extended by caves in which the first hermits of Montmajour no doubt settled.

DAUDET'S WINDMILL
(Bouches-du-Rhône, 11 miles from Saint-Rémy-de-Provence)

«On the road to Arles, at the Fontvieille quarries, beyond Mt. Corde and Montmajour Abbey, on the right-hand side of the road upstream from a large powder-strewn village as white as a stoneyard, stands a hillock covered with pines whose greenery is a refreshing sight in the sunburnt countryside. The sails of a windmill turn slowly in the sky». Alphonse Daudet (1840-1897) described the spot in those terms in the opening to his « Letters from My Mill ».

In fact, Daudet never owned this windmill. He was a guest of the Ambroys at Montauban Castle, and he wrote the book in Paris. Nevertheless, when he went for walks, he liked to stop at the mill and chat to the miller. Today the room on the first floor is open to the public (on show are the stones used for grinding the corn) as is the museum in the basement containing memorabilia of the writer.

One cannot but be impressed by the panoramic view stretching to the Alpilles and Rhône Valley. Nor is the road leading up to the mill in

he shade of some superb parasol
ines devoid of charm.

RLES
Bouches-du-Rhône, 56 miles N-
W. of Marseilles)

Even today Arles is still living
artly in its double-edged past
ased in both Antiquity and the
Christian era. Its glorious history is
written within the modern urban
landscape dominated, from which-
ver direction it is approached,
y the mass of the amphitheatre
nd the square tower of St. Tro-
hime's Church. The town, which
overs the largest geographical
rea of any burgh in France
77,000 ha), has nevertheless mana-
ed to find its niche in the modern
world — it markets rice from the
Camargue and is the setting every
ear for the **International Photo-
raphic Congress** organised by
Lucien Clergue.

In 2,500 B.C. this site between
he Rhône and the Crau Marshes
was already inhabited, even though
. was a totally insalubrious place.
The Phoenicians founded Mar-
eilles c.600 B.C. and at the end of
he same century they settled on the
hill at Arles in order to establish a
trading post there. It was called
« **Théliné** », a Greek word meaning
« nutritive », and it ensured the delta's safety. During the 4th Century
B.C., Celtic tribes founded a town
on the site of the former Théliné,
and its name was transcribed by the
Romans as « Arelate », the « town
near the marshes ». Their aim was
to compete with Marseilles but for
many years Arelate had to be
content with vegetating in the
shade of its rival.

The conquest of Provence by the
Romans in 118 B.C. enabled the
town to develop. Since 120 B.C.
Cimbrians and Teutons had been
leaving the shores of the North Sea
and the Baltic and had been pou-
ring into Provence, after having
first invaded and ransacked the rest
of Gaul. In the year 104, the
Roman Legions grouped on the
borders of the Camargue and La
Crau. While waiting for the arrival
of the enemy, Emperor Marius had
his soldiers dig a canal which was to
connect the town to the Fos Gulf
and guarantee regular supplies of
food by sea for his troops. After the
barbarians' crushing defeat in 103,
Arles, which feared neither silting
up nor flooding by the Rhône,
became a flourishing port with a
number of large shipyards that
were soon to prove particularly
important. When Julius Caesar
tried to bring Marseilles to heel
after it had rallied to his enemy,
Pompei, he obtained twelve ships
within a month from Arles in
49 B.C.! The ships facilitated the
town's capture. As a token of his
gratitude, Caesar founded a
Roman colony in Arles on 21st
September 46 B.C. and granted it
almost all of Marseilles' territory
stretching from the Rhône to the
island of Hyères. Veterans of the
6th Legion settled here. The town
then became a Roman provincial
capital and was given the name
« Julia Paterna Arelate Sextano-
rum ».

Its fortune was made with the
arrival in power of Augustus. The
Roman town was built on the hill
some 90 ft. above the meander in
the river. It comprised a fortified
wall, some fine monuments, and
paved streets laid out like a checker-
board with the forum at the junction of the two main streets, its

Arles, the amphitheatre.

Arles: *tombs in the Alycamps*

temples, amphitheatres, theatres, basilica, and aquaduct from Eygalières 32 miles away bringing an abundant supply of fresh water. Moreover, vast latifundia (large farms) spread over the Camargue and La Crau which were drained and cleaned up. On the right bank beyond a pontoon bridge was the residential suburb of Trinquetaille with its luxurious villas. To the south was the harbour. It should be remembered that, at a time when the town lay nearer the Mediterranean than it does today, the harbour was both for river and maritime traffic and that numerous craft, sometimes from Asia and Africa, tied up there. The town was also a major industrial centre for material, weapons and gold plate. Arles pork meat products, oil and wine from the slopes of the Rhône Valley were also exported. In 306 A.D., after the reorganisation of

Gaul, the Roman Emperor Constantine chose Arles as his place of residence; it stood at the crossroads between Gaul and Italy. The town was improved and was renamed « Gallula Roma Arelas », or « Arles, the small Gallic Rome ». In 313, Constantine set up a large mint there. His descendents kept up an imperial residence in the town.

Christianity, which was introduced to Lyons in the latter part of the 1st Century, gradually gained ground and the first Bishop of Arles, c.225 A.D., was St.Trophime. Because of its political importance, the town was the seat of 19 ecclesiastical councils and it became a veritable religious capital. At the time of the barbarian invasions, from 395 onwards, it was the administrative capital of the Gauls. Arles the Roman city did not really fall until the collapse of the Empire,

when it was occupied by the Visigoths in 455 then by the Ostrogoths before being annexed to the kingdom of the Franks in 536 A.D.

Thereafter, Arles continued to be exposed to every invasion until the 10th Century. In 879, it became the capital of the Kingdom of Arles covering Burgundy and Franche Comté, to which were added Provence and the Vivarais in 933. In the 11th Century, the region was annexed to the Holy Germanic Roman Empire before falling into the hands of the Counts of Provence in the 13th Century and losing its economic importance in the face of competition from Marseilles and its political importance to Aix. It was not until 1481 that the town became part of the kingdom of France. The 18th Century was marked by the terrifying plague epidemic which, in 1720, killed almost half of its 25,000 inhabi-

The Roman theatre in Arles.

PAX AETERNA

DVLCISSIMAE ETIN NOCEN
TISSIM FILIAE CHRYSOGONE IV
NIOR SIRICIO QVAE VIXANN III
M II DIEB XXVII VALERIVS ETCHRY
SOGONE PARENTES FILIAE RARIS
SIMAE ET OMNI TEMPORE VI
TAE SVAE DESIDERANTISSI
M A E

Left: *the Roman baths in Arles.*

Arles: *a tomb in St.Honorat's Church.*

Overleaf: *Arles and the Rhône.*

...ants. With the arrival of the railway in the 19th Century came the end of the commercial river traffic and the glory of Arles. It turned towards mainly agricultural activities.

The Roman town:

As you look at the **ruins of the theatre**, you will have to use a little imagination to conjure up this splendid monument as it once was. Built in the reign of Augustus in the 1st Century A.D., it was unfortunately used as a source of building materials in the 5th Century when St. Trophime's Church was under construction. It fell into ruin, was overrun by houses and gardens and was only rediscovered in the 17th Century.

Today all that remains of the outer wall is a section of the south wall contained in a tower amidst the mediaeval town walls, called **Roland's Tower**. Note, too, the two Corinthian columns (one made of African breccia, the other of Sienna

marble) which backed onto the richly-decorated wall of the stage and flanked the central doorway. There were two other doors to each side, also flanked by pillars. The three levels of one of the 27 series of arches bordering the semi-circle 330 ft in diameter are still visible. Try to imagine the rows of stone steps rising as high as Roland's Tower, 33 rows of them separated into four blocks by flights of steps radiating out from the centre. Only the four lower rows of seats at ground level date from Roman times.

It was at the base of the stage wall that the finest exhibits in the **archaeological museum** were found. Among them was the **gigantic statue of Augustus** almost 10 ft. in height which used to stand in a niche above the central doorway, and the famous « **Venus of Arles** » discovered in 1651, given to Louis XIV in 1683, and preserved since that time in the Louvre after being restored by Giraudon.

Nowadays, in this unusually elegant natural setting, a **Festival** of dance, music, song and drama is held every year in July.

The **amphitheatre**, which is more recent, may perhaps date from the time of the Flavians (70-80 A.D.). Standing like an immense crown at the highest point in the town, the amphitheatre could take up to 20,000 spectators. The gladiators and wild animals have now been replaced by bulls in corridas without killing. The amphitheatre, which fell into disuse in the 5th Century, owes its good state of preservation to its refurbishment as a fortress providing protection against invasion. Since the Saracen period, it has been dominated by the defensive towers to the west, north and east. In the Middle Ages, it was filled with housing and remained so until 1825 when restoration got underway. At that time, there were 212 houses, 1,800 inhabitants, and 2 reliquary chapels. The elliptically-shaped amphithea-

Arles: *the small forum in the Arlaten Museum.*

tre measures 442 ft. by 348 ft. Viewed from outside, it has two storeys of 60 semicircular arches. The austere decoration is Doric on the ground floor and Corinthian on the upper section. The third storey, or attic, which still exists in Nîmes, has completely disappeared here. The other difference between the two is the ground floor gallery roofed in Arles with great slabs of stone while in Nîmes it has semicircular arches.

There were originally four main doorways at the ends of the two through passages, the west door facing the forum being the most important one. Inside, the huge crater comprised 34 rows of stone seats. Note the height of the wall closing off the arena. It used to protect the spectators when the fights included wild animals. Gladiatorial combat, on the other hand, took place on a platform on pillars, bringing it up to 7 1/2 ft. above the present level, opposite the entrances.

In the 4th Century A.D., Emperor Constantine modified the north-western part of the town by having his palace built there. For many years, it was confused with what is still known as the « Palais de la Trouille » (from « trullus » meaning a circular vaulted building). In fact, this was the Roman baths, a vast edifice originally 325 ft. long and 163 ft. wide. To the north near the Rhône, the apse of the **caldarium** (the hot bath) with its barrel-vaulting intact, like the walls in which there are alternating bands of brick and rubble, used to contain a pool paved with marble. Further south is the **tepidarium** (the warm room). The cold rooms, outbuildings, and « palestra » (public gymnasium) all disappeared beneath the housing.

The **forum** dating from the days of Ancient Rome is still the political centre of the modern town. It stood between the Arlatan Museum, the town hall, and the southern end of the present Place du Forum (which in fact runs along only one edge of it), on the least steeply-sloping area of hillside. It looked like a rectangular plot of land surrounded by a portico with three colonnades supported by impressive horseshoe-shaped underground porticos 345 ft. long and 234 ft. wide — the so-called **cryptoporticos** (1st Century B.C.). The entrance is via the Museum of Christian Art. The three sides consist of two parallel cradle-vaulted galleries connected by surbased arches and aired by the vents in the inner gallery. These cryptoporticos were used as corn stores with a view to supplying Rome, and they indicate the town's agricultural and commercial expansion. On the square was a temple dedicated to Rome and Augustus, the cult being confirmed by the discovery in the cryptoporticos of the head of a statue of Octavius as a young man with a beard. The forum also contained a temple on the south side that might have been the Capitol — only two pillars are left, at the corner of the Place du Forum and the rue du Palais. Finally, the baths discovered beneath the Place de la République and a basilica under the Archbishop's Palace completed this group of buildings.

The fine **Christian Archaeological Museum** has been housed since 1815 in St. Anne's Chapel, a Baroque church built in 1629. Many of the exhibits come from the stage wall in the Theatre, in particular the **statue of Augustus**, the goddess with the broken nose, the bas-relief of Winged Victory, and the graceful statue of a dancer. The **Venus of Arles**, which was part of the decoration in the theatre, is now in the Louvre. The bearded head of Octavius, the bust of Tiberius, and the marble shield at the end of the nave, were all found in the cryptoporticos. The very fine mosaics dating from the 2nd and 3rd Centuries A.D. (the « **Four Seasons** », the « **Abduction of Europa** », « **Jason** », and « **Orpheus** ») used to adorn Roman villas in Trinquetaille. Equally admirable are the famous sarcophagi comprising « **Phedre and Hippolytus** » and the « **Hunting Scene** ».

Let us remain on the **Place de la République** where there is a fine Egyptian granite **obelisk** that originally stood in the Roman circus in Arles, a monument which has totally disappeared and which was built in the present-day suburb of La Roquette, 500 yds. south of the town walls. Built first of wood and later, in the Christian era, of stone, the circus was 1,300 ft. long and 325 ft. wide. There were five rows of stone seats catering for almost 15,000 people who came to see chariot races, not trapeze artists or acrobats. A wall, round which teams had to turn, divided the track in two lengthwise and on top of it was the obelisk 49 ft. high. When it had been restored, it was inaugurated with all due ceremony on 20th March 1776 on the present Place de la République.

Still on the square, there is the **town hall** (17th Century) containing the 16th-century **Clock Tower**. Peytret's plans are said to have been redesigned by Mansart. On the ground floor is an admirable flat vault, a fine example of this architectural feature which journeymen completing their Tour of France would come especially to see.

Next to the town hall is **St.Trophime's Cathedral**, showing particularly in the famous portal the harmonious alliance of the Romanesque style and the heritage left by the Romans. Several legends exist as regards St.Trophime's life and identity. He is thought to have been sent to Arles by Rome c.225. In the 12th Century, legend had it that the Bishop of Arles was a cousin of St.Stephen, or perhaps even of St.Paul. As a contemporary of the Apostles, he is said to have brought back from Palestine in 46 A.D. the relics of St. Stephen (which were nevertheless discovered in 425!) and to have founded, in addition to Montmajour Abbey, a shrine to the Virgin Mary in the Alyscamps.

The building stands on the former site of the fifth-century St.Stephen's Basilica which was destroyed during the invasion period and rebuilt in the Carolingian era. In the first decade of the 11th Century, it was again rebuilt to house St.Trophime's relics. Certain sections are still visible low down on the façade. Work began again in 1080. On 29th September

Arles: *Place de l'Hôtel-de-Ville.*

1152, St. Trophime's relics returned to the cathedral and this saint finally supplanted St. Stephen once and for all. Later a portal was built backing onto the west wall, its threshold being raised to provide an additional sense of grandeur to the building overall. This meant that the floor of the church had to be raised in its turn. No doubt everything was finished by 30th July 1178 when the cathedral received a visit from Frederick Barbarossa who came to have himself crowned King of Arles. The final stage of the construction project involved the building of a great three-storey tower topped by an attic based on the one over the Roman amphitheatre. In the 15th Century, the church had to be extended to cater for the large numbers of believers who were drawn to it by the miracles of the Blessed Louis Aleman, Bishop of Arles from 1423 to 1450. The cathedral was enlarged by one-third with a chevet containing an unusually long chancel. As in Les Saintes-Maries-de-la-Mer, the relics were then placed in the tower. In 1632, a door was built on each side of the main portal. The two stained glass windows at the transept crossing date from 1695. During the Revolution, the cathedral became a Temple of Reason and escaped damage. In 1801, it was attached to the Bishopric of Aix-en-Provence and thereafter St. Trophime's became a mere parish church. It was classified as a Historic Monument by Prosper Mérimée.

The **portal**, not unlike the one in Saint-Gilles, is a masterpiece of Provençal Romanesque architecture. The firm lines and wealth of ornamentation make this arch topped by a pediment a veritable triumphal arch reminiscent of the one in Saint-Rémy. On the Tympanum, which depicts the Last Judgement, Christ is seated in majesty —crowned, and dressed in a finely-draped mantle, He is seated within a mandorla (a celestial almond-shaped halo) at the base of which is a smaller oval representing the world. He has raised His right hand in benediction and is surrounded by the symbols of the Evangelists and flanked by angles in adoration on the arching. On the lower section is the procession of the chosen few to the right of Christ while the rejected are shown on His left chained together by a demon. The two groups are separated by the frieze bearing carvings of the Twelve Apostles on the lintel above the door. Below are exemplary scenes from the Childhood of Christ topped by statues of the nine Saints of the Church. This provides the harmonious association of ancient forms and Christian themes.

And so to the interior. St. Trophime's astonishes visitors because of the height of the nave (over 65 ft.) and the narrowness of the side aisles with half-barrel vaults. The nave has a broken barrel vault resting on ribbed arches, and is lit by tall semicircular windows. Only two decorations break the overall austerity — a cornice of acanthus leaves at the base of the vaulting and the capitals on the pillars. Above the transept crossing is a dome lit by four semicircular windows. The Gothic chancel and its apse lead into a ambulatory that opens onto eight radiating chapels.

Arles: *the entrance to St. Honorat's.*

Right: *the Romanesque portal in St. Trophime's in Arles.*

Arles: *a capital in the cloisters in St. Trophime's.*

Right: *the cloisters and belltower in St. Trophime'.*

The church contains some fine sarcophagi from the latter years of the 4th Century including a magnificent one used as an altar bearing a continuous frieze illustrating the **crossing of the Red Sea**. The wall in the left-hand side aisle is covered with Aubusson tapestries depicting scenes from the life of the Virgin Mary.

The **cloisters in St. Trophime's** are the most famous in Provence because of the abundance of carvings. With overall dimensions of 91 ft. by 81 ft., they were originally used by the cathedral's Canons as a place in which to take a stroll and were surrounded on all sides by living quarters. They illustrate the happy juxtaposition of two very different architectural styles — the north and east galleries are Romanesque (12th-century barrel vaulting) while the south and west galleries are Gothic (14th-century vaulting on ogival ribs). The capitals on the twinned pillars all show either foliage or scenes from the

Old and New Testaments or Provençal legend. The pillars that alternate with the colonettes are decorated with large statues and bas-reliefs. The cloisters owe their elegance more particularly to a technique taken from Roman architecture. The Romanesque galleries **are roofed with barrel-**vaulting which is higher on the out-side wall than on the arches so that one's eye is automatically drawn towards the light in the garth, emphasising the decorated colonnade. Note the work on the statues, the gravity of their faces, the clothes and sandals that in some cases are reminiscent of Antique Art. Note, too, the north-west pillar which is absolutely faultless —St. Trophime is in the centre flanked by St. Peter and St. John. Between the pilasters, two bas-reliefs depict Christ's Resurrection and the saints of Bethany buying aromatic herbs.

It is, though, in the **Alyscamps** that the connection between

Roman tradition and Romanesqu grandeur is most evident. The plac is protected by **St. Honorat' Church** and it keeps watch ove pagan and Christian dead alike The word « Alyscamps » come from the Latin « Elysei Campi » the Elysian Fields which were th home of the blessed dead of Anti quity. From the Roman perioc until the late Middle Ages, this wa the most famous cemetery in the Western world. The vast graveyarc owes its fame to St. Genest, the Clerk of the Court who refused tc transcribe a persecution orde condemning Christians to death During the invasions in the 4tl Century, his relics were transferrec to the Roman cemetery beneath the present Church of St. Honorat. A increasing numbers of believer also wished to be buried there, the graveyard was extended further and further and the Alyscamp were covered in sarcophagi, with the most ornate tombs lining the Roman road. At that time, the

cemetery contained some fifteen churches and chapels. Of the monastery founded by St. Césaire in the 6th Century before transferring it to a site inside the town walls, all that remains is a fine semicircular arch.

Numerous legends grew up around the Alyscamps. It was said, for example, that St. Trophime was the founder of the Christian cemetery. People went so far as to say that they could see the mark left by Christ's knee when He came to bless the Alyscamps in a church in what is now the Genouillade District. Some of the sarcophagi were believed to have been filled with water capable of working miracles. Then again, the Alyscamps were said to be the burial ground of the knights of Roncevalles. Ariosto also describes how the sarcophagi came up out of the ground to welcome the dead after a battle between Charlemagne and the Saracens. Dante himself mentioned this field of dead in the lines of his « Inferno ».

Unfortunately, the graveyard was pillaged by the lords of Arles who had no hesitation in making presents of the sarcophagi to important guests, and by monks who used the stones to build churches and monasteries. A boat destined for Charles IX sank in 1554 with all its precious cargo on board. After the pillaging of the Revolution, the construction of the railway brought about ultimate ruin. All that is left today is one path lined with monolithic sarcophagi, leading to St. Honorat's.

The name of the Dutch-born painter, Vincent Van Gogh (1853-1890) is closely linked to this town. He arrived in Arles in 1888 « to see another kind of light... to see this stronger type of sun ». His paintings then became a continuous stream of sunshine. Sometimes he would paint gigantic sunflowers; sometimes it would be the portrait of a postman or a zouave. The artist Gauguin came to join him from October to December 1888, and this encouraged him to create more decorative compositions, especially on the canvases dealing with the Alyscamps. Their life together, though, came to a tragic end on 24th December — after having tried to attack his friend with a razor during his first fit of insanity Van Gogh returned to his room and cut his ear off.

Fortunately, there are a number of sarcophagi in the **Museum of Christian Art** which is housed in a fine 17th-century Jesuit church. It is second only to the Latran Museum in Rome for the number of sarcophagi in its possession. The marble tombs dating from the 4th and 5th Centuries are unusual for their Classical inspiration from Rome and its adaptation to the requirements of the Christian religion. A large amount of space is left for the illustration of Biblical scenes or pictures of daily life. Note the three sarcophagi (4th Century) which were uncovered during archaeological digs in Trinquetaille in 1974.

Other museums of interest are the **Réattu** and the **Arlaten**. The former is housed in what was originally the great Priory of the Knights of Malta, not far from the Roman baths of Constantine's era. It has belonged to the town of Arles since 1867. The Renaissance mansion with its courtyard decorated with a balustraded staircase, was

Arles: *general view of the Alyscamps.*

The Romanesque façade of Saint-Gilles-du-Gard.

bought by the local artist Réattu whose works, all strongly academic in style, are on show here. The museum also has an exhibition of paintings by Antoine Raspal, a local portrait artist who died in 1811. One of the rooms contains memorabilia of the Order of Malta. The museum owns a fine series of 16th-century Flemish tapestries, the « Wonders of the World ». Many modern and contemporary artists are also represented — Picasso, Léger, tapestries by Lurçat, sculptures by Bourdelle, Zadkine, etc. A photographic exhibition is held in the museum every year.

The **Arlaten Museum** set up by Frédéric Mistral in the former Laval-Castellane Palace using the money from his Nobel Prize for Literature in 1905, has brought together a collection of Provençal traditions, arts and crafts. Tools, costumes, furniture and engravings retell the story of the Camargue and La Crau, the work and day-to-day existence of the men who live between river and marsh. There is also a reconstitution of a herdsman's hut and various scenes from Provençal life. This is an opportunity to admire the splendid local costume of the women of Arles, immortalised in a famous painting by Van Gogh (November 1888) — a long straight skirt with a narrow box-pleat, a shawl draped across the so-called « chapelle » decorated with jewellery, and the velvet ribbon on the plaited chignon.

SAINT-GILLES-DU-GARD
(Gard, 10 miles W. of Arles)

The small town of Saint-Gilles-du-Gard, which lies in a rich agricultural area (fruit, cereal crops, Costières wines) owes its fame mainly to a former abbey church well-known for its very fine façade that bears comparison with that of St. Trophime's in Arles.

As soon as the origin of this town is discussed, hypotheses are rife. Some people believe that it was once a port, « Heraklea », founded by the Phoenicians. Indeed, during the Revolution, it took the name of Héraclée. Its history is closely-linked to the legend surrounding the life of St. Gilles, a hermit of Greek origin who doubtless lived in the 8th Century and who was a follower of St. Gregory, Bishop of Arles. He left Greece on board a ship which brought him to Provence. Legend has it that a doe which was being run to earth took refuge in his cave and that he protected the animal from the hunter's arrow with his hand. The huntsman, shaken by his miracle, is then said to have decided to found an abbey on the site. During a trip to Rome, St. Gilles received from the Pope two carved doors which he hastily threw into the Tiber. They floated down to the sea, followed the course of the minor Rhône, and

were washed ashore in front of the cave. The saint was buried in the church that he had built and became the object of a cult.

The powerful abbey reached its heyday in the 11th and 12th Centuries when it was one of the stages on the pilgrimage to Compostella. At that time, the town had a population of 30,000 and the abbey was placed under the protection of the kings of France and the Pope. Thereafter, at the time of the Albigensian heresy, it went into a swift decline. The heresy gained a strong hold on Languedoc and Pope Innocent III ordered a Crusade to stamp it out in 1209. It was in this abbey that Raimond VI, Count of Toulouse, received orders from the Pope through one of his representatives to fight this sect. However, the papal legate, Pierre de Castelanu, was assassinated at the door by one of the Count's equerries. The nobleman was then excommunicated. He had to submit after swearing obedience to the Pope on 12th June 1209 and after having been whipped, naked. That did not prevent him from rebelling again at a later date and unsuccessfully fighting the crusaders led by Simon de Montfort. In 1562, during the Wars of Religion, the abbey's monks were thrown into the well in the crypt and the monastery was set ablaze. After the destruction of the great belltower in 1622, all that remained of the Romanesque minster was the façade. The present church, which is much smaller than the original, was built in 1655.

The 12th-century façade includes three magnificently-carved doorways by artists from several different schools — local sculptors who finished the statues of the Apostles, artists from the Toulouse school who created the main portal, others from the Paris Basin who worked on the side doors. The tympana above the side doors depict the **Adoration of the Magi** and the **Crucifixion**, flanking a **Christ in Majesty** (above the main door), while the **Passion** and **Resurrection** form a long frieze linking the three tympana.

The **crypt**, 162 ft. long and 81 ft. wide, no longer has its ribbed vaulting but it still comprises very old ogival arches (mid 12th Century). This is where the saint's tomb is to be found. The former chancel, which stands outwith the present church, is now in ruins.

Also open to the public is a **Romanesque house** dating from the 12th Century where Guy Foulque was born; he became Pope in the 13th Century under the name of Clement IV.

Left: *statues on the façade of Saint-Gilles-du-Gard.*

A bas-relief on the façade of Saint-Gilles-du-Gard.

THE CAMARGUE
(Bouches-du-Rhône, 19 miles S. of Arles)

A visit to the Camargue is an opportunity to see nature untouched by man, and there is now a preservation order on the area. It has a mass of very varied flora including halophytes (plants adapted to life in a salt environments), particularly around the Vaccarès Lake and the **Rièges Islands** where you can see, among others, red behen, saltwort (green in the spring, grey in summer, and red in winter), sea-purslane, tamarisk, and zinnias. In addition, there are large numbers of birds in the **Pont-de-Gau Ornithological Park** and the **Vaccarès Zoological and Botanical Reserve**. As long ago as 1928, the State opened a reserve covering an area of some 13,500 hectares in which bird and plant life are protected. Ducks and teal from northern Europe take refuge here in the winter, and in spring and autumn many birds (heron, Passeriformes, egrets etc.) stop here during migration. Pink flamingos can be seen in the region during the summer months.

It is impossible to describe this area without mentioning the horses, the bulls and the « gardians ». The **camargue** is a horse of 13 or 14 hands. And what about its appearance? It has a large square head, short ears wide at the base and set well apart, slightly-protruding eyes, a thick mane, a pale grey coat, a deep chest and short neck, and a long tail. It is a very hardy animal, both agile and brave, and its origins are open to question.

As for the **gardian**, he is no theatrical cowboy; he is an excellent horsemen doing a difficult and physically hard job. On St. George's Day (he is their patron saint), a Mass, games, and processions are organised in the Camargue and in Arles. On that occasion, the gardian carries a trident rather than the pole that he uses in his everyday job.

And so to the **black Camargue bull**, recognisable for its lyre-

A horse in the Camargue marshes.

shaped horns. Again it is difficult to trace its origins. In any case, the pure breed died out almost a century ago. The local term, « manade », refers to the herd of bulls a person owns, and to everything connected with the raising of the herd — land, pastures, horses and gardians. Nowadays, a herd consists of a maximum of 150-300 head of cattle and there are about forty of them in all. And did you know that there were some 16,000 bulls in 1600 and only 1,800 in 1900? In the spring, they are branded on the rump with their owner's name, during the so-called « ferrades ». Visitors can see branding in operation at the **Domaine de Méjanes** near the Vaccarès Lake.

The bulls are also the stars of the « cockade races ». While a bull in an arena dies within 15-20 minutes of being taken out of the pen, the animals taking part in the unrestricted Provençal race die a natural death, after a career lasting 7, 8 or 10 years. Men play with them but do not slaughter them.

AIGUES-MORTES
(Gard, 28 miles S. of Arles)

To the west of the Camargue, in a landscape of saltpans and canals (the Rhône-Sète Canal) stands the beautiful walled town of Aigues-Mortes which looks as if it has stepped straight out of the Middle Ages. Its name, quite the opposite of the town of Aigues-Vives which is also in the Gard, comes from the Latin, « Aquae Mortae », meaning « dead waters ».

In 1240, the King of France, St. Louis, acquired the small village of Aigues-Mortes from the monks in the nearby abbey of Psalmody. At that time, it was connected to the Mediterranean by a narrow channel called the « Grau Louis ». The king needed a place on the Mediterranean coast as the point of departure for his projected crusade. Aigues-Mortes quickly became a prosperous harbour protected by the **Constance Tower** and by a wall which the king's son, Philip III, was to complete. In 1270, despite opposition from his entourage because of his failing health, the king set out from Aigues-Mortes on a new crusade but he died of the plague soon after disembarking at Carthage. The last important date in the town's history was 1418, during the One Hundred Years' War. The Burgundians captured the town which was then besieged by the Armagnac faction. Some of their supporters within the walls managed to overwhelm the garrison in one of the gates, thereafter enabling the attackers to undertake a verit-able massacre. All the Burgundians slaughtered were placed in one of the towers later called the **Burgundians' Tower** and, in order to avoid decomposition, their bodies were preserved in salt. This is the origin of the expression « bourguignons salés » (salted Burgundians) in a popular song of the day.

The regularly advancing coastline and the silting up of the channels led to the town's gradual decline, which became final in the 18th Century when the port of Sète was founded. Nowadays, the vineyards and saltpans are the mainstays of its economy.

The quadrilateral walls of Aigues-Mortes are topped by a parapet walk and flanked by a number of towers (the Burgundians' Tower, Villeneuve, the Wick, the Salt Tower, etc.). Although the walls have only two gates on the north side, there are five in the south wall facing the wharves.

The mighty Constance Tower, which has been connected to the ramparts by a bridge since the 16th Century, was used as a prison for five hundred years during which time it housed Knights Templars, great lords who opposed their king, Protestants and political prisoners. From the top of the watchtower, which served as a lighthouse from the 13th to the 16th Century, there is a vast panoramic view over the town, the surrounding plain, the Cévennes ridge, the South of France saltpans, and the Camargue.

LES SAINTES-MARIE-DE-LA-MER
(Bouches-du-Rhône, 24 miles W., of Arles)

Now situated right on the Mediterranean near the mouth of the minor Rhône (whereas it was once

The ramparts around Aigues-Mortes in the Camargue.

several miles inland), the tiny port of Les Saintes-Maries-de-la-Mer is world famous as a place of unusual religious faith and the symbol of gipsy peoples everywhere.

In the early Middle Ages, the area was quite different to what it is today; it probably looked more like the marshland round Poitiers. It was, in fact, a group of wooded green islands separated by small branches of the river.

In the 6th Century, a small chapel was no doubt built, the « Sancta Maria de Ratis » or « St. Mary of the Island », which was given to the monks from Montmajour Abbey in 1078. It remained in their possession until the 17th Century. It was most probably in the 12th Century that St. Mary of the Island became Our Lady of the Sea (Notre-Dame-de-la-Mer), a name which it was to keep for many a long year. The 12th-century monks integrated the original chapel into a new, very plain church flanked on the north side by a square belltower leading straight into the chancel. At the end of the 14th Century, when the coastline was plagued by pirates, the village developed round about and the church had to be fortified. The thick village walls were demolished during the Revolution so that today's visitors can fully appreciate the very special appearance of the church. From that time onwards, Notre-Dame-de-la-Mer became a resting-place for pilgrims and the monks, like their colleagues throughout the mediaeval world, had no hesitation in inventing legends of the saints to attract the crowds, telling the tale of Mary-Jacob, the Virgin Mary's sister, and Mary-Salome, the mother of James, son of Alphaeus, and John the Evangelist. Provençal tradition has it, with absolute disregard for any historical fact, that c.40 A.D. the two saints were abandoned with their companions (one of whom was Sara, their Black servant, whose name is written without an 'h' as it is not Biblical in origin) out at sea by the Jews of Jerusalem in a boat with no sail or oars and without any food or water. Thanks to the protection of the Almighty, the boat drifted ashore on the beach at the foot of the present church. Later, once they had built a shrine to the Virgin Mary, these disciples of Christ went their separate ways in order to bring Christianity to Provence, with the exception of the two saints and Sara.

It was, though, on the initiative of King René that the place really gained its universal fame. On 3rd December 1488, according to an official document, the Good King René who had obtained from Pope Nicolas V the right to explore the chapel, uncovered beneath the entrance to the present crypt « unbroken bowls, pieces of coal, and ashes » as well as numerous pieces of pottery bearing Christian motifs. He also found a section of sarcophagus which is now used as an altar, and a fragment of polished marble called the « saints' pillow ». Most importantly, though, Nicolas de Brancas, Bishop of Marseilles, drew up an official document attesting to the discovery of two skeletons buried in the earth, one of them with arms crossed. Was it an ancient dwelling which just happened to be on the site of the church? Or was it a forgotten grave from the early Middle Ages? Nobody is in a position to make any categorial statements these days, but there was absolutely no doubt in the minds of those who discovered it — the skeletons could not be anything but the bodies of the holy women.

Later, King René ordered alterations and improvements to the church. As the original chapel had been destroyed during the dig, the nave was extended by two spans and a crypt was excavated, which meant that the chancel had to be raised. An upper chapel was set out in which the reliquaries of the saints were put on show. Yet it was not until the 19th Century that the village officially became known as Les Saintes-Maries-de-la-Mer.

Without anybody really knowing when, how, and why, Sara became as much the object of worship as the two saints, and the gipsy folk who had been attending pilgrimages since the 15th Century recently accepted her as their patron saint. Her position as a servant and her wanderings throughout the Mediterranean region must have appealed to this nomadic people on the outer edge of society, a group treated with suspicion. Since that time, who pilgrimages, one for the Feast Day of Mary Salome on 22nd October and the other for Mary Jacob on 25th May, attract a large crowd of gipsies and pilgrims. After covering it with flowers, they carry down to the sea a statue of Sara which is usually on show in the crypt. On the following day it is the turn of the saints' boat, which stands in the third arch inside the church during the rest of the year. This is also an opportunity for popular festivities, given the presence of the gardians from the Camargue — there are farandoles, bull-brandings, and horse-and bull-racing.

THE CHATEAU D'IF
(Off Marseilles, Bouches-du-Rhône)

The port of Marseilles lies beyond a barrier of small islands which close off the harbour entrance — **Ratonneau, Pomègues,** and **If** (measuring 217 yds. by 182 yds.), the most famous of the three. It is open to question whether it owes its name to the yew trees (« if » in French) that are said to have covered it in days gone by. One thing, though, is sure — the islands off Marseilles were neither deserted nor completely devoid of vegetation in the past. Hunting was even a fruitful occupation.

On 20th December 1524, three months after the end of the Siege of Marseilles by Charles V's troops, building began on the **Château d'If,** a square with sides 91 ft. long protected by towers on three sides only. **St. Christopher's,** the most

Left: *the fortified church in Les Saintes-Maries-de-la-Mer.*

Overleaf: *the Château d'If.*

massive of these towers and also the tallest at 72 ft., faces seawards past Ratonneau while the other two, **St. Jaume** and **Mangouvert**, look towards the harbour. The chroniclers of the day noted that the fortress was built without the consent of the people of Marseilles. Should the town decide to revolt against the King of France, it would be extremely difficult to hope for assistance from the sea. Despite their opposition, the fort was completed in July 1531 and a garrison of 200 men was billetted there. On several occasions, it was to provide excellent protection for Marseilles.

On 4th March 1660, there were celebrations in the château! King Louis XIV had come to visit it, accompanied by his cousin, Mademoiselle de Montpensier. The illustrious guests were received with much pomp by the governor of the fortress. « A great buffet was set out but, as it was Lent, few ate there ». In 1860, another V.I.P. visited the château in the person of Mme de Grignan.

Rather than a place for refined entertainment, however, the Château d'If was first and foremost a prison that was usually full, where the prisoners lived in extremely miserable conditions. Vauban wrote, after inspecting the main tower, that he was « unable to see inside the others because of the prisoners who were in them ». Many Protestants (Jean Serres, Elie Neau, etc) conspirators, and political opponents, Mirabeau, and the Marquis de Sade, were all « detained » there, for varying lengths of time.

The most famous prisoner in the Château d'If, though, was the more or less imaginary hero of a novel by Alexandre Dumas, « *The Count of Monte Cristo* », published in 1846. Edmond Dantès, unjustly imprisoned as a supporter of Napoleon Bonaparte, was said to have met Father Faria there. Who could forget how the two characters prepared their escape for many months until, one day, the priest died. The sad event gave his companion a brilliant idea — he took the place of the dead body in the sack that was then thrown into the sea. All he had to do was tear his way out of his canvas prison and swim to freedom and wealth (he had been told about a fabulous treasure buried on the island of Monte Cristo).

Marseilles: *Notre-Dame-de-la-Garde.*

Made a listed building in 1926, the Château d'If belonged to the Army until the end of the Second World War. Nowadays, it is part of a much larger complex, the permanent leisure centre created in 1970 by Marseilles City Council.

BASILICA OF NOTRE-DAME-DE-LA-GARDE
(Marseilles, Bouches-du-Rhône)

All over the world, as soon as Marseilles is mentioned, what immediately springs to mind is **the Canebière**, the most famous street in the city, the old **harbour** and its thick forest of pleasure craft, and the «Good Mother», an expression which shows how fond the locals are of Notre-Dame-de-la-Garde. It is a veritable symbol of the Phocean town and was built in the mid

107

19th Century on a spur of rock 526 ft. above the sea. There is no better place from which to get a magnificent panoramic view of Marseilles, the offshore islands, and the Estaque and Etoile ranges.

From time immemorial, the people of Marseilles had built shrines dedicated to the Virgin Mary on this spot, before erecting a chapel in the 15th Century to which a fourth aisle was added in 1833.

Twenty years later, the architect Espérandieu was to build on the site the basilica we see today, in the Romanesque Byzantine style that was then in fashion and which hi master Vaudoyer had already use for the Cathédrale de la Majo (1852-1893).

The thing that immediatel strikes visitors is the richness an diversity of materials used — pre cious marble, onyx, granite, an

Marseilles: *a statue of the « Good Mother » in the basilica*

Aix-en-Provence: *the Place de la Rotonde.*

...osaics. The numerous votive offe-
...ings in the crypt show the grati-
...ude of the working classes for the
...iracles worked by the Good
...other whose gilded statue (32 ft.
...igh) has stood on the tower since
...867. Every year on 15th August,
...n impressively-large crowd of pil-
...rims converges on the cathedral;
...hey come from all over Provence.

...IX-EN-PROVENCE

...Bouches-du-Rhône, 18 miles N-E.
...f Marseilles)

The former residence of the
...ounts of Provence has the rare
...rivilege of being able to satisfy the
...xpectations both of students and
...usic-lovers and of holidaymakers
...r people taking the waters. It is no
...xaggeration to say that the attrac-
...on of « the Athens of Southern
...rance » (as Frédéric Mistral put it)
...not only its delightful setting and
...s tranquillity but also the wealth
...f architecture and the intense cul-

tural activity. This town of historical monuments, shaded walks, and
fountains has a university (with
almost 15,000 students) and, since
1948, has been the home of the
International Music Festival. It has
nevertheless not remained static
amidst its prestigious past, as
shown by its increasing population
— from 30,000 inhabitants in 1921,
to almost 120,000 today, with a cor-
responding increase in the town's
residential requirements after the
opening of the factory complex in
Fos. The spa is also a major centre
of ready-prepared almonds, some
of which are used to make the
famous calisson sweet.

Founded in 123 B.C., Aix was
originally no more than a Roman
encampment whose construction
had been ordered by Consul Sextius Calvinus, the victor of the
Celto-Ligurians in Entremont (a
mile-and-a-half to the north). The
garrison was set up to the south of

the Gallic fortress, not far from the
hot springs with thermal properties
called « Aquae Sextiae » in Latin, or
the « waters of Sextius ». Aix was
born.

Having been ransacked by the
Lombards in the 6th Century and
later by the Saracens, it has no
Roman remains, unlike Arles,
Nîmes, or Orange. In 1189, when it
became the capital of the Counts of
Provence who held a brilliant court
there, its population increased dra-
matically and large-scale building
sites came into being. Yet, ruined
by plague epidemics (particularly
the one which killed half its inhabitants between 1348 and 1361) and
by the intrigues fomented at the
Court in Naples, Aix had to wait
for the reign of the « Good King
René » (1434-1480) before it regai-
ned its taste for dynamic
development.

This cultivated and much-
travelled Duke of Anjou, who did

Aix-en-Provence: *an 18th-century mansion overlooking the Cours Mirabeau.*
Left: *the town hall fountain, Aix-en-Provence.*

Overleaf: *the Cours Mirabeau.*

ot finally settle in Aix until 1471 nce all hope of ever reigning over ne Kingdom of Naples was dead, ttached himself to the task of eforming the administrative structure and economic revival of his ountry with no little show of intelgence. Yet it is his image as organier of celebrations and ournaments, and as patron of the rts surrounded by a court of rtists, which best describes him. He was to write a variety of works ncluding his famous «Livre du œur d'amour épris» (Book of the Heart bound by Love) which he robably illuminated himself and which is kept in the **Méjanes Library**. This library, opened in 870, occupies several rooms in the own hall and houses an collection f some 170,000 books. In quite nother vein, the king encouraged he cultivation of carnations, roses nd the Muscat grape in Provence.

Throughout the 15th Century, Aix was continually being altered and improved; the present **Place des Prêcheurs** was laid out in front of the Count's Palace and the final arch of the cathedral was completed.

On 11th December 1481, with the death of his successor, Charles III of Maine, who bequeathed Provence to the King of France, this period of independence and prosperity came to an end. The capital of a sovereign province then became merely one of the kingdom's provincial capitals, although it did enjoy a large measure of autonomy and certain privileges. Aix remained the residence of the governor and in 1501 King Louis XII founded assizes and a Court of Accounts there. In spite of numerous political struggles which shook the town in the 17th and 18th Centuries, Aix continued to

undergo improvements. During the reign of Louis XIV, three noteworthy types of building project came into being — the creation of a vast new district by **Archbishop Michel de Mazarin**, the opening in 1651 of what we now know as the **Cours Mirabeau**, and the building of numerous private mansions. In the 18th Century, several squares were laid out, including the beautiful **Place d'Albertas**. The **Cours Mirabeau** serves as a reminder of the popular revolutionary speaker Honoré Gabriel Riqueti, Count of Mirabeau. After a turbulent youth (his family nicknamed him Mr. Squall or Mr. Hurricane), this passionate orator whose face was deformed by a badly-treated case of smallpox was elected to represent Aix' Third Estate in 1789. When the Revolution came, or to be precise in the space of a single night (4th August 1789), Aix lost its

position as provincial capital. All that was left was its scholastic, university and cultural rôles which it defended bitterly and to which it gave even more prominence than before.

The Cours Mirabeau on the site of the old town walls offers the shade of its four lines of young elms to strollers attracted by the numerous shops, bookshops and cafés that line one side. One of them, the **Café des Deux-Garçons**, is particularly famous; it used to be frequented by large numbers of artists and writers e.g. Zola, Giraudoux, Jouvet, Cendrars and Cocteau. This major thoroughfare along which «people of quality take the air in their carriages in the afternoons and on foot in the evenings» (Marquis de Préchac) has a particularly harmonious layout, for the designers were careful to make it wider at the end than at the entrance. Magnificent private mansions with fine carved doors and wrought-iron balconies resting on caryatides or telamones by the Puget school add to the charm of this central avenue. There are also several fountains to admire — the **Fontaine des Neuf-Canons** (Nine Cannons) in the centre, the spring water fountain at the entrance to the Rue Clémenceau, and **King René's Fountain** at the end of the avenue. No.55 used to be the hatter's belonging to **Paul Cézanne's** father; the artist was born in 1839 at no.28 Rue de l'Opéra. When he reached adulthood, this great painter of local landscapes used to frequent the Café Clément on the ground floor of the Gassendi Residence and he would go to his studio via the avenue which now bears his name (originally called the Chemin des Lauves). He died on 23rd October 1903 at his home in 28 Rue Boulegon.

St. Saviour's Cathedral, which is said to have replaced a Roman temple to Apollo, is a composite building showing every architectural style in fashion between the 5th and the 17th Centuries. Its layout is based on the Latin Cross, i.e. there is a nave and two side aisles in addition to a transept and an apse. The right-hand aisle and the adjoining cloisters (built between 1160 and 1180) are evidence of the vitality of Romanesque architecture in the Aix region. The absence of vaulting explains the lightness and elegance of the cloisters whose arches rest on fine twin colonnettes with capitals decorated with pictorial scene or foliage.

A door in the north-west corner of the cloisters leads into the cathe-

Right: the cloisters in St.Saviour's, Aix-en-Provence.

Aix-en-Provence: *the pediment on the Corn Exchange.*

dral. In the first chapel is St. Mître's tomb, a 5th-century white marble sarcophagus. A little further along is the **baptistery**, an octagonal structure composed of an ambulatory roofed with 12th-century Romanesque arching, eight pillars with Corinthian capitals thought to date from the days of Ancient Rome and to have been re-used here, a 16th-century dome, and an octagonal baptismal font in the centre. It is believed to be a very old monument, perhaps dating from the Merovingian Period (5th Century), although it has undergone numerous alterations over the centuries.

In the vast Gothic nave is the famous **Triptych of the Burning Bush** painted in 1476 by the King's favourite artist, Nicolas Froment. Shown in the company of Queen Joan of Laval at prayer and contemplating the Mystery of the Virginity of Mary (symbolised by the Bible story of the bush which remained green as it burned), King René, dressed in the austere habit of the monks of Saint-Victor, was then 67 years of age. The Flamboyant Gothic façade is enriched by the doors in its 16th-century portal made by Jean Guiraumond from Toulon. On the left stands the Gothic tower (14th-15th Century). Only two of the statues are original — **St. Michael slaying the dragon**, above the main window, and the **Virgin Mary** on the pier.

Other churches are also worth a visit:

The **Church of St. John of Malta**, the first Gothic building dating from the late 13th Century. This was the original chapel in the former priory of the Knights of Malta. Today it houses the tombs of the last Counts of Provence.

The **Church of St. Mary Magdalen**, built in the Baroque style in the 17th Century, has a very large canvas attributed to Rubens in the left arm of the transept. At the end of the right-hand aisle, in the fourth chapel, is an 18th-century marble statue of the Virgin Mary. The real treasure, however, is the central panel of the **triptych of the Annunciation** in the left-hand aisle near the altar to Our-Lady-of-Grace. This work, created by an anonymous arist, was ordered by a rich member of the middle classes, Pierre Corpici. A magnificent **reliquary** contains the bones of the Blessed André Abellon, a member of the Order of Preaching Friars (1450).

The architectural beauty of Aix is not restricted to religious buildings; the **Place de l'Hôtel de Ville** indicates a will to treat the utilita-

On previous pages: *the courtyard of the town hall, Aix-en-Provence.*
Right: *the triptych in St. Saviour's Cathedral, Aix-en-Provence.*

Aix-en-Provence: *the Four Dolphin Foutain.*

The Montagne Sainte-Victoire.

ian warehouse of the **Corn Market** is a work of art (its pediment, decorated by Chastel, symbolises the rivers Rhône and Durance) and to improve the new open space by decorating it with a fountain designed by Le Brun. The **town hall**, with its clocktower that was originally the 16th-century belfry, dates from the 17th Century. On the first floor are the **Méjanes Library** and the **Saint-John-Perse Foundation**.

Other squares are equally noteworthy, and all are decorated with fountains. There is the **Place des Prêcheurs** (1758) with its great fountain built by Chastel, the **Place des Quatre-Dauphins** and its fountain (1665) which is the pride of the Mazarin District, and the finest of them all the **Place d'Albertas** opened in 1745 by Jean Baptiste to the south of the mansion that his father, Henri Reynaud d'Albertas,

President of the Court of Accounts, had built in 1707.

THE SAINTE-VICTOIRE
(Bouches-du-Rhône, 4 miles E. of Aix-en-Provence)

It would be a pity to visit Aix without taking a day trip into the surrounding countryside, following in the footsteps of the painter Paul Cézanne. Just a few miles out of town is the grey luminous limestone ridge of the **Montagne Sainte-Victoire** which culminates in the **Pic des Mouches** (3,286 ft.). This barren yet fascinating landscape, which was immortalised on more than one occasion by the artist, belongs to the same range as the **Sainte-Baume** and the **Trévaresse**. The south-facing slope of the Sainte-Victoire overlooking the **Arc Valley** is a sheer wall of rock while to the north a series of limestone plateaux

slope gently down to the Durance Plain. The name of the ridge is also associated with the victory of Marius' legions over the Cimbrians and Teutons en route for Rome in 102 B.C.

You may care to begin your trip with a visit to the **Bimont Dam** built in the midst of wooded countryside across the R. Infernet which flows along the foot of the Sainte-Victoire. Tourists who are not put off by physical effort can then go to **Les Cabassols** and follow a shepherd's track which will take them, in under two hours, to the priory of **Notre-Dame-de-Sainte-Victoire** (alt. 2,925 ft.), a place of pilgrimage that is always busy.

You can go on to the 55-foot high **Cross of Provence** (alt. 3,071 ft.). From the platform, there is a vast panoramic view over the mountains of Provence — Sainte-

The Château de Vauvenargues.

Relief features in Provence

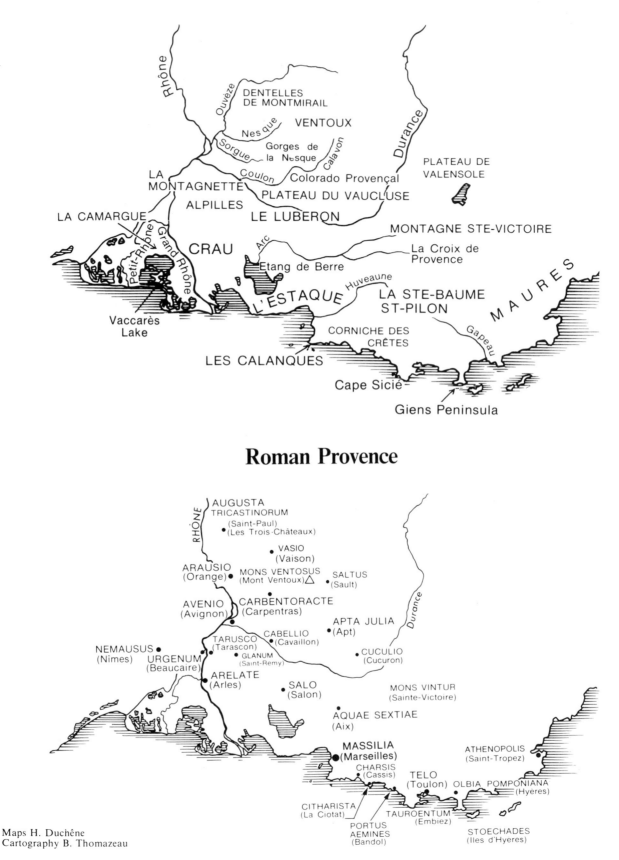

Rhône

Ouvèze

DENTELLES
DE MONTMIRAIL

VENTOUX

Nesque

Durance

Sorgue

Gorges de
la Nesque

Calavon

PLATEAU DE
VALENSOLE

Coulon

Colorado Provençal

LA
MONTAGNETTE

PLATEAU DU VAUCLUSE

ALPILLES

LE LUBERON

LA CAMARGUE

MONTAGNE STE-VICTOIRE

Petit-Rhône

Grand Rhône

CRAU

Arc

La Croix de
Provence

Etang de Berre

MAURES

Vaccarès
Lake

L'ESTAQUE

Huveaune

LA STE-BAUME
ST-PILON

Gapeau

CORNICHE DES
CRÊTES

LES CALANQUES

Cape Sicié

Giens Peninsula

Roman Provence

AUGUSTA
TRICASTINORUM
(Saint-Paul)
(Les Trois-Châteaux)

RHÔNE

VASIO
(Vaison)

ARAUSIO
(Orange)

MONS VENTOSUS
(Mont Ventoux)△

SALTUS
(Sault)

AVENIO
(Avignon)

CARBENTORACTE
(Carpentras)

Durance

APTA JULIA
(Apt)

NEMAUSUS
(Nîmes)

TARUSCO
(Tarascon)

CABELLIO
(Cavaillon)

CUCULIO
(Cucuron)

URGENUM
(Beaucaire)

GLANUM
(Saint-Remy)

ARELATE
(Arles)

SALO
(Salon)

MONS VINTUR
(Sainte-Victoire)

AQUAE SEXTIAE
(Aix)

MASSILIA
(Marseilles)

ATHENOPOLIS
(Saint-Tropez)

CHARSIS
(Cassis)

TELO
(Toulon)

OLBIA POMPONIANA
(Hyères)

CITHARISTA
(La Ciotat)

TAUROENTUM
(Embiez)

STOECHADES
(Iles d'Hyères)

PORTUS
AEMINES
(Bandol)

Maps H. Duchêne
Cartography B. Thomazeau

Main châteaux, castles and churches in Provence

Key

⊙ **Château or castle**

• **Church**

A pastoral scene in Provence.

aume, Etoile, Vitrolles, La Crau, e Durance Valley, the Lubéron, e Alps of Provence, and the Pic s Mouches.

On the way back down, a stop in **Vauvenargues** is a must. It is well-known because of the castle built on a spur of rock (17th Century) and because of the fame of its last owner, the painter Picasso, who is buried in the grounds.

ft: fishermen in the old harbour in Marseilles.

Layout of Provençal churches

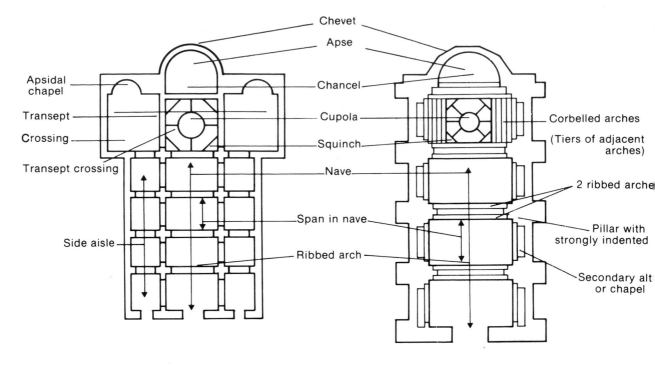

The layout of Provençal churches is sometimes based on the Latin Cross...

... but more often the church has a single aisle and no transept.

Often the side aisles are extended beyond the transept, forming the ambulatory which runs rounds the chancel. Sm chapels called apsidal chapels open onto the ambulatory.